SO-CBM-816

Personal Journeys

52 Weekly Devotions on Life, Love, and Faith

By Dean Salter

Stillmeadow Press

Copyright © 2008 Dean Salter

All rights reserved. Reproduction or utilization of this work in any form, by any means now known or hereinafter invented, including but not limited to, xerography, photocopying and recording, and in any known storage and retrieval system is forbidden without permission from the copyright holder.

Library and Archives Canada Cataloguing in Publication
Salter, Dean
    Personal Journeys: 52 weekly devotions on life, love and faith / Dean Salter
ISBN 978-0-7795-0239-4
    1. Devotional literature, Canadian (English). I. Title
BV4832.3.S24 2008   242   C2008-901997-0

Printed in Canada, By Blitzprint Inc.

Published by:
Stillmeadow Press
78 Tucker Circle
Okotoks, Alberta
T1S 2J7

To the memory of Bill and Alice Salter and
Ray and Barbara Leask.

You always had wonderful stories to tell.

Introduction

———◆·◆·◆———

Welcome to *Personal Journeys*. This book reflects my own personal journey, my day-to-day struggle to make sense of the "big ideas" of *life, love,* and *faith.* I claim no brilliant insight and no recondite body of knowledge that would make me uniquely qualified to discuss these "big ideas." I'm not even a Hollywood celebrity, which would, of course, qualify me to speak authoritatively on all subjects known to humanity. Like you, I'm a unique human being on a unique life journey. I experience this journey and reflect on it from my own little corner of the world and I think that's the value of this book. Most of our journeys aren't grand, but they're still totally real and vitally important to ourselves and the world around us. They bear reflection. *Personal Journeys* is full of small stories. They're often just modest but memorable events that have happened to me over the years which have unexpectedly opened up some new ways of reflecting on the world. I offer them in the hope that they might connect with you and your own stories in a special way; a way that opens up some fresh insights for you into the confusing, delightful, and miraculous world of life, love, and faith.

Most of the "personal journeys" in this book first appeared in my column for the *Guelph Mercury* newspaper entitled (not surprisingly) "A Personal Journey:". My thanks to the *Mercury* for permitting these ramblings over the period of five years in their weekend edition. There are also a few "journeys" here that are drawn from a column I wrote for a delightful (now-defunct) Waterloo, Ontario newspaper called *Footprints*, plus some material specially written for this book.

Personal Journeys is designed as a 52-week devotional guide for either individuals or small groups to use in whatever creative ways they see fit. Each journey is tied to a Bible passage that is designed to place the "little event" into a broader and richer context. There are many appropriate passages (the Bible, after all, is a treasure of insights into the nature of life, love, and faith). I simply chose one relevant passage for each week. I've also included questions for reflection and/or discussion, which I encourage you to alter or expand upon as you feel the need.

Finally, there is an opportunity to pray and encouragement to act. Devotional material seems rather bereft, doesn't it, if it's just a gaggle of words which doesn't encourage us into something positive and dynamic in our lives?

This is a 52-week resource designed for those of us who follow the Christian faith. The problem that you'll find with such a resource is that somewhere along the line Christian power brokers had the temerity to allow Easter to float around on the calendar. So I'd encourage you to float Palm Sunday and Easter into the appropriate weeks for the year in which you're using this book and then fill in the empty spaces.

May God bless you with bountiful thoughts and more than a few "off the wall" insights as you connect your personal journey with mine and try to make sense of those "big ideas" of life, love, and faith.

Dean Salter

Week 1: Scratch That Itch — Get Involved

When Jesus returned to his hometown of Nazareth as a respected itinerant preacher, he went to the synagogue for worship and was invited to read from the scroll of the great prophet Isaiah. It is often said that this is the moment when Jesus announces the active, dynamic thrust of his entire ministry. His will be a spirit-filled ministry oriented towards bringing new life and hope to those in the community who are poor or sick or abused or for whatever reason pushed to the far edges of society. Jesus won't sit back and wait. He'll actively engage his world with his abilities to preach, teach, and heal. He also warns his former hometown that you don't receive the Kingdom of God by some kind of divine right. You receive it because you actively seek to do God's will. Jesus' dynamic ministry is a template for our own life of service to our communities.

...and the scroll of the prophet Isaiah was given to him. He unrolled the scroll and found the place where it was written: "The Spirit of the Lord is upon me, because he has anointed me to bring good news to the poor. He has sent me to proclaim release to the captives and recovery of sight to the blind, to let the oppressed go free, to proclaim the year of the Lord's favor." (Luke 4: 17-19)

A Personal Journey:

I'm always on the lookout for little scraps of information that I think are critical indicators of our planet's health and well-being. You can imagine my shock and dismay over a radio news report which trumpeted the fact that over the past year there have been 31 percent more UFO sightings in Canada.

With more leisure time throughout the universe we should probably expect more visitors. The "visiting" is not the source of my dismay. The thing that upsets me is that alien abductions have taken a sharp nosedive! Apparently, far fewer people are being hoisted up to the Mother Ship than in previous years. So, my question is: What are we, chopped liver? Aliens are content to cruise around the planet at a safe distance, but they don't want to talk with us anymore? They don't care what we have to say? This is, indeed, a sad state of affairs. Arms-length tourism is a very depressing trend.

I don't want to be too critical of our intergalactic friends. Admittedly, earth people can be difficult at times and, no doubt, they've had some bad experiences with a few cranky abductees. But, that's no reason to give up! I'm sure there are lots of nice people on the planet who'd give their eye teeth to spend a weekend on the Mother Ship.

Ironically, our outer space visitors seem to have fallen into the same rut as many of us earthlings. We are more and more content to be isolated and disconnected from our neighbours and our community. Staying aloof from the people and events of our town is not difficult. We can easily be consumed by work; by the impositions of cell phones, computers, and PDAs. It's all too easy to consider our town as a "bedroom community" and nothing more.

But, of course, our town *is* something more. It's the community in which we live. No community can be healthy if it's comprised of people who essentially don't care about it. Eventually, such neglect will ruin the quality of life for everyone. A community of observers is a failed community.

Years ago, when I was living in Saskatchewan, I was handed a pretty fair civics lesson from a man I was working with in Yorkton. He said it's absolutely critical for anyone who cares about living in a healthy community to read the local newspaper. That's where you find out what's happening around you and why. That's how you get a deeper sense of who your neighbours are and what they care about. That's how you get a sense of what programs and services your community has and what's lacking. The local newspaper can provide the information to inspire, frustrate, or cajole us into getting involved. It creates, in its own unique way, an itch that needs to be scratched.

It's important to celebrate and support the local media whether it's the newspaper, magazines, radio, or television. They have very talented people who let us know what's happening in our communities and why.

Of course, following the local media isn't the same as getting involved. It's just a vital window into the opportunities that exist. As I said above, it creates an itch that needs to be scratched. But, it can't make us scratch! Motivation comes from within; from a genuine sense that life is better when community is better. I believe the local media provides a trail for us to follow towards healthy involvement in government, politics, religion, sports, community service organizations, environmental and other advocacy groups, and a host of other community-healthy endeavours.

The challenge to all of us (including all you intergalactic visitors) is to move from benign observation to active engagement with the people and events around us.

A Time for Reflection:

If you had to stand up before your entire community and tell them what your personal "ministry" is in the world, what would you say to them?

What is it in ourselves or in the community that seems to limit us from living out the ministry we feel "called" and "equipped" to perform?

How can we break down the barricades that separate us from our neighbours and which keep us from getting involved in our communities?

How much do you actually know about your local community and where do you get your information? If you wanted to help, would you know where to start?

If you were to look deep inside yourself, what would you find that motivates you to reach out to those in need?

A Time for Prayer:

Gracious God, as we take our first steps into a New Year, help us to remember that we are not walking alone. We are part of a neighbourhood. We are part of a community. Guide us to understand that you've gifted us with ministries of service in a world that cries out for healing. Give us the courage to define those ministries for ourselves and to live them each day in our community. Amen.

A Time for Action:

Each great journey begins with a first step. Totally commit yourself this year to a volunteer activity that you feel is consistent with living out your ministry in the community and the world. Stick with it and consistently think about what this work means to you—and to others.

Week 2: Shall We Gather at the River?

———————◆◦◆◦◆———————

Jesus often used parables to teach profound lessons about the Kingdom of God. The technique was commonly used by rabbis of his day to place their messages in contexts that people would understand—contexts drawn from their daily lives. The parables made reference to such common scenarios as shepherding, farming, fishing, cooking, and commerce. Each scenario was a metaphor that gave people a little more insight into what the Kingdom of God required of them.

The parable of the sower (Matthew 13: 1-9), for example, carries a powerful message to both individuals and to the organized church throughout history. It says the Kingdom of God cannot be received by those who have not done the work of preparation. If there is no ready foundation from which people can open their arms and receive the Kingdom, then the Good News, the messages of peace, justice, hope, love, and abundant life can't get through. Nothing happens unless the people are ready for something to happen. The parable has clear importance to the church, the "body" of Christ, which must help prepare people to hear the Good News. In fact, the message is so important for the future church that Matthew punctuates this section of his gospel with a full explanation of the parable of the sower.

"Hear then the parable of the sower. When anyone hears the word of the kingdom and does not

understand it, the evil one comes down and snatches away what is sown in the heart; this is what was sown on the path. As for what was sown on rocky ground, this is the one who hears the word and immediately receives it with joy; yet such a person has no root, but endures only for a while, and when trouble or persecution arises on account of the word, that person immediately falls away. As for what was sown among thorns, this is the one who hears the word, but the cares of the world and the lure of wealth choke the word, and it yields nothing. But as for what was sown on good soil, this is the one who hears the word and understands it, who indeed bears fruit and yields, in one case a hundredfold, in another sixty, and in another thirty." (Matthew 13: 18-23)

A Personal Journey:

You've all, no doubt, heard the story about the firebrand young minister who preached a wildly enthusiastic sermon on the evils of "demon rum." At the end of his scorching diatribe against alcohol he shouted out, "If I had all the beer in the world, I'd take it and pour it into the river." Not certain if he'd made his point strongly enough, he shouted even more loudly, "And if I had all the wine in the world, I'd take it and pour it in the river." Finally, caught up in the excitement of his own voice, the young preacher shook his fists wildly in the air and screamed, "And if I had all the whiskey in the world, I'd take it and pour it into the river."

On the edge of apoplexy, his point driven home, the preacher fell back exhausted into his chair. The song leader, a long-time member who had seen many ministers come and go, then rose to his feet with a smile and announced the hymn. "For our closing song," he said, "let's sing Hymn 365, *Shall We Gather at the River.*"

I've always thought that one of organized religion's greatest failings is that it's always trying to tell people what to do. Like the young preacher above, the church can offer a truckload of "thou shalt nots" that cover virtually every aspect of life on this planet. The Bible is held up as the great "rule book" which will confirm how wrong we are to follow every instinct we've ever had.

For some people, of course, having a long list of "thou shalt nots" works just fine. They're looking for a hard set of rules which will keep life simple and straightforward for them. But, the vast majority of people aren't prepared to blindly follow a set of restrictions simply because someone up in a pulpit claims they must. People can be ornery that way. If the church orders them to refrain from alcohol, tobacco, idle gossip, and bad-mouthing the neighbours, they may say "Amen" in worship but in real life they'll ask "why?"

Most churches don't have a very good answer to the 'why' question. Just accept it, they say. It's in the book...those are the rules.

And that's the problem, really. Following religious rule books is like trying to eat your way out of an endless vat of gelatin. No matter how much you eat you're surrounded by still more. It all belongs to someone else and you don't even know why you're there except that you can't think of any other place to be. There's nothing firm to stand on; there's no solid ground for you; nothing to think about except eating more gelatin.

If organized religion has any meaning today it's not as the guardian of a hoary rule book which eliminates the need for personal decision-making. Instead, the church should be helping people build platforms they can stand on. For example, instead of dated interdictions against everything from "demon rum" to "the wandering eye," the church needs to challenge people to understand social justice from a Christian perspective and build a life platform based on that understanding. Understanding inter-personal relations can lead to a platform built on fairness and trust. Understanding the peace of Christ can lead to a platform built on self-sacrifice rather than self-indulgence.

My point here is that rule book religion is a dead end. At the end of the day, all we have are a long set of "thou shalt nots" that are external to our lives. We're waiting to be told what to do next by those to whom we've surrendered the task of moral thinking. Either that, or we tune it out altogether. And, neither response is good enough. Faith requires more. The church needs to dig out of the "thou shalt not" mentality and help people build moral and ethical platforms which are intrinsic to their lives. Once a platform of understanding is built, people can view every life situation, whether political, social, economic, or inter-personal, from the vantage point it allows them. A solid platform encourages self-directed decisions based on the depth of a person's own spirit and faith.

It's time to cut our losses and put an end to rule book religion. It's time for the revolution. It's time for people to take control of their own faith, enjoy a fresh walk with God, and build the platforms they can stand on for life in this challenging new millennium.

Right now, I'm trying to decide whether I should follow the rest of the crowd down to the river.

A Time for Reflection:
Read the parable of the sower and the biblical passage explaining it. Discuss what it means to grow in "good soil" in this world. Where do you find yourself

most often in this story (like seed on the bare path, on rocky ground, among thorns, in good soil?) Why are you there?

Have you ever looked upon the Bible as a book of rules? How has that helped you in your faith development? How has it hindered you?

If the minister in the pulpit clearly lays down the rules for you to follow in life, do you follow them?

What does it mean to build moral and ethical platforms from which you can view life, make decisions, and take action? How are such platforms built? Who is involved in the "construction?" Do you think such platforms are valuable? Necessary?

Who would you prefer to help you build your moral and ethical platforms? A mentor? The body of the church? Christ in private reflection? Christ in public worship?

A Time for Prayer:

Gracious God, guide us to be fully open to the power of your wisdom. Through the power of the Holy Spirit may we have the strength to seek out the good soil of peace, justice, hope, love, and abundant life in which to grow our lives. Empower us, God, to take counsel and grow in wisdom so that your great and gracious Kingdom lives and breathes within us and we know in our hearts the pathways that we must take. Amen.

A Time for Action:

Build a platform for social justice. Read the Bible. Talk to your minister, your teacher, your family, a trusted friend, and/or a person you consider a mentor about what they fundamentally believe constitutes social justice in the world. Develop a statement that outlines the cornerstones of social justice for you;

principles for which you'd "go to the wall." Think about where this statement leads you and follow your heart.

Week 3: Sitting Down in the Middle of the Road

It's would be easy to see "The Beatitudes" as a rather pretty set of rules that would guide us to the good life, if they weren't so difficult to follow on a day to day basis. In the early days of his ministry, Jesus gathered his disciples on a mountain top away from the larger crowds and instructed them in the ways of God's world by giving them The Beatitudes. In fact, they're not intended as an overly hopeful guidebook to the good life. They are evidence of what the world will be like when the great Kingdom of God is brought to full fruition. These are the "blesseds" of a world to come, a world where all heads bow to God and all spirits unite with the Divine. It's a world that will come only as we find it in our hearts to follow God's will.

...Blessed are those who hunger and thirst for righteousness, for they will be filled. Blessed are the merciful, for they will receive mercy. Blessed are the pure in heart, for they will see God. Blessed are the peacemakers, for they will be called children of God... (Matthew 5: 6-9)

A Personal Journey:

Over the last couple of weeks I've been reading Michael Moore's bestseller, *Stupid White Men*. Written a few years ago, it's a biting commentary about the disastrous state of a world that's been run for too long by "stupid white men." Moore's incisive rant makes you want to laugh and cry at the same time over the lack of common sense (and common decency) that plunges our planet repeatedly into chaos.

One thing about *Stupid White Men* that particularly strikes me is Moore's prescription for bringing about change in the world. He says that the best way to effect change is to sit down in the middle of some important road to somewhere and refuse to move. This gets the attention of the "powers that be." If it's done often enough by enough people "the powers that be" get very anxious because all sorts of people start to notice. As more and more people start to notice, "the powers that be" are forced to do something to stop all these people from messing up the traffic flow. And, in the end, nobody moves (and none of the onlookers are satisfied) until "the powers that be" actually do the right thing.

Non-violent action has brought about some amazing changes in our world. Think of Martin Luther King Jr. or Mahatma Gandhi or Nelson Mandela as three pretty good examples of what happens when people decide to sit down in the road and say, "OK, here we are. Now deal with us—over and over again in increasing numbers." They taught us if we don't find a way to sit down in the road, "the powers that be" will not be confronted by the demands of justice. If we don't sit down in the road we have simply acquiesced. King, Gandhi, and Mandela never acquiesced.

The idea of sitting in the middle of some important road and refusing to budge hasn't gone away. Hundreds of thousands of people worldwide, myself included, have done just that in recent years to protest the immoral, pointless, and increasingly disastrous war in Iraq. Opponents of the war, now a solid majority worldwide, are making a difference.

Governments don't like it when large numbers of people sit down in the streets and refuse to go away until plans and policies change, and justice is done.

They don't like the idea that more and more people will come and sit down if governments can't find a better way to conduct foreign policy than through war and violence. Non-violent protest is, once again, attracting the attention of "the powers that be."

It strikes me that while sitting down in some important road and refusing to budge is an important strategy for group action, it also speaks to us personally. More often than not, we try as hard as we can to outrun our personal issues and problems. We ignore them; we shuffle them to the back of our consciousness; we work harder and play harder in the hope that they'll go away. We carry the same attitudes toward personal problems that we do with global concerns. If we run fast enough, we won't notice them so much and there's a chance they'll resolve themselves.

Denial never seems to be a good strategy, whether it has to do with Iraq or our own personal lives. As strange as it sounds, maybe it's a good idea sometimes to sit down right in the middle of our own personal road (a very important road) and non-violently refuse to budge. Refuse to budge, that is, until we're sure the right thing is going to get done— and we know how to do it. In fact, it seems doubtful that we can apply this strategy globally if we can't apply it personally.

Sitting down in the middle of some important road and refusing to budge can be a dangerous strategy for change. It requires taking a risk of life and limb. But, whether we do it personally or corporately or both, the results are irresistible. "The powers that be" will have no choice but to cave in.

Things will change. The right thing can get done.

A Time for Reflection:
Think about non-violence as a life strategy. What's in your heart right now that draws you to non-

violence? What's in your heart that points you in another direction?

In God's great Kingdom the "peacemakers" will be blessed. What do you think is the true spirit of a peacemaker? Can you think of times in your life when you've had the opportunity to be a peacemaker? What was your spirit at the time and what did you do?

Do you think you could actually sit in the middle of some important road and refuse to budge if you felt it was God's call to help create a better world?

As a person of faith, how do you feel when "the powers that be" come into clear conflict with the demands of God's Kingdom? What's your initial reaction? Your long-term response?

Are you non-violent with yourself? Are you non-violent with the world around you? Where is God in your life and where is the power of The Beatitudes?

A Time for Prayer:

Loving God, teach us to open our hearts and minds to the vast possibilities of your Kingdom. Help us to hear your call in the day to day processes of our lives and to be of such powerful spirit that we can hunger and thirst for righteousness, that we can be merciful in all things, pure in heart, and committed to all things which make for peace in our world. Gracious God, guide us to a faith that advances your Kingdom through both prayer and action. Amen.

A Time for Action:

Where do you see injustice in your community, your nation, and your world right now? What is God saying to you about getting involved as a lover of peace and righteousness? If God has guided you to one place, find a way to literally or figuratively sit in the middle of some important road until "the powers that be" take notice and "the right thing gets done."

Week 4: Is God on Our Side?

In the Old Testament, Job has been afflicted with unimaginable losses. He has lost wealth, home, family, and health. These things, he feels, should have been protected by God, for Job has always been a good and faithful man and certainly deserves none of the ruin that's afflicting him. Why is God not being God? Why isn't He living up to expectations? As you can imagine, Job has some choice words for a God who has let him down so badly. Then, at the critical moment, God speaks, and, in the majesty of the moment, we begin to realize that so often what we worship isn't God at all.

Then the Lord answered Job out of the whirlwind: "Who is this that darkens counsel by words without knowledge? Gird up your loins like a man, I will question you, and you shall declare to me. Where were you when I laid the foundation of the earth? Tell me if you have understanding. Who determined its measurements—surely you know! Or who stretched the line upon it? On what were its bases sunk, or who laid its cornerstone when the morning stars sang together and all the heavenly beings shouted for joy?" (Job 38: 1-7)

A Personal Journey:
In my younger days, I can remember attending a sports banquet where the guest of honour was a

moderately successful National Football League quarterback. At some point, late in his career, he had "found religion." At least, that's what the brochure of the Christian group sponsoring the banquet trumpeted in big, bold letters. He had "**FOUND RELIGION**." But, to hear him speak, it sounded as if he'd found some kind of magic elixir to help him throw better passes and win more football games.

This aging athlete peppered his keynote address with examples of how God had guided his throwing arm to complete 12 passes in a row; how the Divine Being had not allowed him to throw an interception in four games; and how the Benevolent One was on his side as he single-handedly led his team into the playoffs.

When you're at a sports banquet and not inclined towards deep, analytical thought, this type of speech often goes by with little comment. After all, at least you've heard of this guy—and he *is* a professional athlete! But, in hindsight, if you like to take your religion with a dash of reflection and a pinch of common sense, this man's use of God was troubling.

Was God really on his side? Is God such a partisan football fan that he (or she) would quietly tamper with the physiology of one player and one team in order to guarantee them victory over another? What heinous sins has the other team committed that God is so pointedly *not* on their side?

I realize I'm being far too judgmental, but I have to wonder if that almost famous quarterback had actually found religion at all. An elixir, perhaps. A psychological prop to extend his career. But, not religious faith. At the same time, at least he was sniffing around the whole concept of faith, and that's not a bad thing. Maybe somewhere down the road this man who "found religion" will allow a deeper religious faith to find him.

My point here is that the whole concept of God being on our side is frought with danger and disappointment. If I believed God was exclusively "on my side" I'd have to come up with some awfully good reasons why. And I'd have to explain why God had clearly chosen not to be on "the other side." Are my opponents really that irredeemably evil that God would make the rather un-God-like decision to totally abandon them?

What if God is *not* on our side? How would it affect our lives as a people of faith if we came to the conclusion that God was not on our side? I'm sure there's some small heresy involved here, but I think we'd all be better off!

God is *not* on my side. But, then again, God isn't on your side either. In fact, what if we came to believe that God doesn't take sides—that "taking sides" isn't God language at all? We'd have to stop believing in God as some kind of performance-enhancing elixir that gives us the edge in a competitive world. We'd have to think of God differently.

What if we came to see God as a "surrounding spirit", a wonderful "other" that seeks to wrap every one of us in hope, love, and boundless potential, and calls on us to communicate and connect in life-giving ways with the world around us? No winners and no losers. No sides. Just a unity of creation gifted with boundless potential.

History has proven over and over again that when God is "made" to take sides, our planet is placed in harm's way. A God who doesn't take sides is a God in whom we can find the seeds of peace.

A Time for Reflection:
What good is a God who doesn't protect us from heartbreak and failure? Why should we believe in a

God who doesn't give us the edge we need to win our daily battles?

If God doesn't offer "success" what *does* He/She offer to us? What does it mean to really know God at the deepest level?

How does it feel to live in a world where God is not on your side? How will you pray?

If God doesn't take sides, what does it mean to live faithfully in a complex, interconnected, multicultural, multifaith world?

A Time for Prayer:

Gracious God, I am Job. I'm angry that you have not spared me from anguish, pain, and loss. I'm angry that you have not lived up to my expectations; that you have not honoured my goodness with good things. Gracious God, I'm the athlete who assumes he has bought your loyalty and power with the standard formulas of faith. I am the one who believes you can be controlled by my will and my needs. I am the one who doesn't believe you are God at all; who cannot comprehend your mysteries, your majesty, and your plan. Gracious God, open me to the healing, compelling wonders of a God who is not on my side. Amen.

A Time for Action:

What will you do differently today in a world where God does not take sides? Think of an "opponent" in new ways, as if God was a "surrounding spirit" wrapping you both together in life. Work in your heart, mind, and actions to eliminate the word "opponent" for this person or group and find a new direction for this relationship.

Week 5: Is "Community" a Dead Duck?

Through the power of the Holy Spirit and consumed by Jesus' life, death, and resurrection, his little band of disciples stayed together. In time, largely through the compelling energy of their leader, Peter, the little band of believers started to grow into a much larger community of faith. There is no question that this diverse group of personalities which grew into the Early Church took "community" very seriously. If you were part of the community of Christ, you'd have entered the door with great courage and you'd have taken the membership responsibilities very, very seriously. This community of Christ wasn't an afterthought for them. It was the centre of their lives. It's where they found fellowship, and hope for the future.

All who believed were together and had all things in common; they would sell their possessions and goods and distribute the proceeds to all, as any had need. Day by day they spent much time together in the temple, they broke bread at home and ate their food with glad and generous hearts, praising God and having the goodwill of all the people. And day by day the Lord added to their number those who were being saved. (Acts 2: 44-47)

A Personal Journey:

When did we decide that "community" doesn't matter anymore? Does anybody remember the day that happened? Was there an e-mail about it that I missed?

One of the most disturbing trends in our society today is the headlong rush to curtail or eliminate the activities that humanize our workplaces and our institutions. More and more, those things which create community are being sacrificed on the altar of expediency and a misguided conception of cost-efficiency.

The corporate world leads the way. Despite copious amounts of literature that expound on the valuable bottom line of community, most businesses are headed the other way. The perks that make it "good to work here" are being picked off one by one.

Due to accounting costs, the cafeteria is now "pay as you go," which keeps the old crowd away. The company Christmas party is dropped in favour of smaller, less costly gatherings, and everyone goes home early. The picnic is dropped and the annual bus trip to a Blue Jays game is cancelled.

Slowly, all activities that don't fit neatly into a profit centre are eliminated. Community is proudly dismantled as if it's a sign of progress.

Tipping their hats to the business world, governments have tried to strip our school systems of their community values. Fretting about money and liability, they've targeted after-school activities for the chopping block. The very things that teach young people how to be together and work together for a common purpose are obviously no longer important to our leaders. These activities are, apparently, neither expedient nor cost-efficient in the creation of a high-tech workforce.

Very soon our governments will need to show us their vision for a future in which no one understands either the joys or the responsibilities of living in a community.

Even those who espouse a religious faith are increasingly turning away from communities where faith is expressed. Many religious souls find it expedient to "blue sky" their faith. 'I don't need to go to church because I see God in the hills, the trees, the birds, the flowers, and the bubble gum on the bottom of my running shoe,' they say.

Once again, community is put down as unimportant. The values we teach and learn from one another in church—the nurture, the service, the stewardship, the challenges, the mystery of a shared sacrament—all these are hard to find in the "blue sky." But many people would rather search the "blue sky" than enter the "body" of Christ, the community of the church.

What happens to a society that ceases to value itself as a builder of communities? What happens when the humanizing, uniting culture of our workplaces and institutions is slowly stripped bare by a harsher culture of expediency and cost-efficiency? Isn't it a slow march towards a future which is more of a nightmare than a dream?

A Time for Reflection:

What communities are you active in and what do you see as the value of community in your life? What can you draw from community that you can't draw from being in a quiet place reading a good book?

How do you see your communities (your workplace, your town or city, your schools, your church, your volunteer activities) changing since you first joined them?

How do these changes make you feel?

Draw a picture in your mind of what a future world without genuine "community" would be like. How would people behave? What would we believe?

Where do you see hope in all this? Where do you see community growing right now? Who is fighting for community in our world at the present moment? What can you do to keep your vision of community alive and well?

A Time for Prayer:

Gracious God, forgive us. We've sold out to money, power, fear, and expediency. In order to keep the focus on ourselves and our desire for more and more material things, we've sold out the communities in which we live. Slowly, inexorably, we've given the nod of approval as more and more of the underpinnings of healthy community have been knocked away in the name of cost-efficiency. Loving God, help us to remember the spirit-filled power of the Early Church. Help us recapture a vision for the future in which community overcomes selfishness and our hands are held open in friendship rather than curled greedily around our own possessions. Amen.

A Time for Action:

Where you see the potential loss of community at work, school, or in the general community, start a petition. The "powers that be" prefer to make community-destroying changes quietly with little involvement from others. Ensure that this doesn't happen.

Do something to create community. Organize a picnic or a show or a golf tournament—something that brings people together. Take positive steps to counter the efforts you see in your workplace, school, town, or church to devalue community. If not you, then who?

Week 6: To Evolve or Not to Evolve (Is That the Question?)

When the Apostle Paul traveled to Athens on one of his missionary journeys, he was shocked at the Gentile population's unbridled fixation with idols and idol worship. For him, this intellectual centre felt like the heartland of paganism. It would be a "tough sell" to proclaim Christianity to this group, but it was important to try. The question remained: how would he do it? Certainly he couldn't use the same images he would use in talking with local Jewish communities which were scattered throughout the Roman world. He needed to "communicate" differently. He needed to connect with this curious Gentile crowd, using images they could understand. So he talked about the "Unknown God," a concept Athenians were familiar with. This Unknown God has now been revealed, he said. Now, let me tell you all about it...

In one brilliant moment, Paul "communicated." He connected Christianity with a religious concept that was already part of the Athenians' world view. He found common ground and won the respect of many who wanted to hear more about this new faith.

Then Paul stood in front of the Areopagus and said, "Athenians, I see how extremely religious you are in every way. For, as I went through the city and looked carefully at the objects of your worship, I found among them an altar with the inscription, 'to an unknown god.' What therefore you worship as unknown, this I proclaim to you. The God who made the world and everything in it, he who is Lord of heaven and earth, does not live in shrines made by human hands, nor is he served by human hands, as though he needed anything, since he himself gives to all mortals life and breath and all things." (Acts 17: 22-25)

A Personal Journey:

We just need to accept it. There are some aspects of life on this planet that have evolved much faster than we have. As a result, no one can really understand these things anymore—if they ever could. Canadian elections and Stephen Harper are two good examples. But, by far, the best example is television advertising.

Now that I'm dieting again, I can't chase out to the fridge every time there's a commercial on the TV. So, I'm forced to sit there and take in the wonder that is modern advertising. And, it *is* a wonder!

Was it that long ago when you could watch a TV commercial and actually know right away what product was being sold? Was it so long ago when a TV ad actually mentioned the product by name and even gave us a few sketchy ideas as to why we should buy it?

Apparently, the "Advanced Life Forms" who control advertising have decided it must evolve from the humdrum presentation of a product to the evanescent glimpse of an IDEA, shimmering in the ether. If most of the population sits drooling in their easy chairs saying, "Whaaaa...wuzzzz...aaaat?," that's not really an advertising problem. It's a problem of human evolution.

Case in point: Not so long ago, I spent 30 seconds watching a commercial where men were playing basketball on an outside court somewhere in the world. When the 30 seconds were over, I still didn't know if I was being sold shoes, t-shirts, basketballs, soft drinks, or tickets for the NBA. I had even less idea why I should buy any one of these things. The words and music offered no clues.

Case in point: A sleek, black car careens down a mountain road at night. Every once in awhile you get a quick look at the car, which really doesn't matter, since most cars look alike these days. There is, of course, a sleek, beautiful woman in the car. And, for some reason, there's a train with mysterious people in it. When the ad was over I wasn't sure whether to race out and buy the latest fragrance, the car, the beautiful woman's dress, or tickets on VIA Rail. The words and music offered no clues.

It's a mystery to those of us who are unevolved.

In fact, can't you just see a brace of advertising gurus sitting in their meditation room viewing the first cut of a new ad? "This is a noble effort, Grasshopper, but you have spent too much of your time focusing on the bra. What is the IDEA of the bra? What is the ESSENCE of the bra? If they *see* the bra, they'll know immediately that the ad is *about* the bra. Our ad will lose its mystery, people will cease to be confused. Remember Grasshopper, not the bra but the IDEA and ESSENCE of the bra."

There is, apparently, no going back, particularly where evolution is concerned. It remains for we, "The Unevolved," when trapped in front of the TV during a commercial, to utter the only rallying cry we have left in a harsh world that no longer wishes to communicate with us: "Whaaaa...wuzzzz...aaaat?"

A Time for Reflection:

Think about a time when you and a friend, acquaintance, spouse, or partner miscommunicated. What caused it? How did you feel about it? What impact did it have on your relationship?

Can you name five or more ways to ensure that miscommunication doesn't happen if the above situation should arise again?

What did Paul do differently in order to reach the people of Athens with his message about God and Jesus Christ? What does his approach mean to you when discussing your faith with non-Christians today?

What is the difference between the advertising described in "A Personal Journey:" above and the methods used by Paul to reach the people of Athens? Are they both manipulations?

Is it acceptable to confuse or stretch the truth in the name of a good cause? Think about what it means in our day and age to communicate with integrity.

A Time for Prayer:

Loving God, guide us to talk with one another in the power of your good spirit. Help us communicate in a way that shows your love for truth and justice and for our brothers and sisters who share your world. May our words bring understanding. May we speak with integrity and may our words bring healing and peace to bear on the brokenness around us. Guide us, we pray, to share the gospel in ways that bring life to the world. Amen.

A Time for Action:

Has there been a time in your life when words have broken a relationship? Think and pray about the words that could heal that relationship again. Find a gentle, non-threatening way to use them.

Through your church or another group, organize or join a program of interfaith dialogue. Discover and celebrate the things which we, as Christians, hold in common with those of other faiths.

Week 7: The Best Gift of All

The story of the rich young man in the gospels is a real shocker for those of us living in wealthy North America. Here's a man who seems to be prime disciple material. He's a fine and upright person who scrupulously obeys the commandments and seems to want nothing more than to do the right thing, gain favour with God, and inherit eternal life.

He's also *very* wealthy and Jesus knows something about the man's wealth that he himself doesn't understand. Wealth is a great barrier in this young man's life. It keeps him from being everything he can be. It stands in the way of him truly giving himself to God. His attachment to Mammon is too great for him to truly give himself to anything else, not even the God he thinks he adores. When the moment of decision comes, he sadly leaves the field and wanders back to the self-involved, comfortable life he's always known. For 2,000 years the rich young man has stood as the archetype of what it means to let the world tie us up in knots when Jesus says, "Come, follow me."

As he was setting out on a journey, a man ran up and knelt before him, and asked him, "Good Teacher, what must I do to inherit eternal life?" Jesus said to him, "Why do you call me good? No one is good but God alone. You know the commandments: 'You shall not murder; You shall not commit adultery; You shall not steal; You shall not bear false witness; You shall not defraud;

Honour your father and mother.'" He said to him, "Teacher, I have kept all these since my youth." Jesus, looking at him, loved him and said, "You lack one thing; go, sell what you own, and give the money to the poor, and you will have treasure in heaven; then come, follow me." When he heard this, he was shocked and went away grieving, for he had many possessions. (Mark 10: 17-22)

A Personal Journey:

Many years ago, I was invited to teach a university course about mass media. I can remember my first-ever lecture like it was yesterday. I had prepared a brilliant set of lecture notes on the exciting topic of "media bias." Admittedly, the notes were a bit brief and cryptic—but brilliant nonetheless. I was confident I could expound on this topic at great length. No problem.

Fifteen minutes into the 50-minute class I'd pretty much exhausted my knowledge of "media bias." Actually, I was effectively out of new information in 10 minutes. After checking my watch, I decided to do a slow recap, which added another five. Questions didn't materialize as I'd hoped. In a quiet panic, I said, "O.K., so now I want you to talk among yourselves." Which they did—for the last 35 minutes.

I mention this because it just so happens that my turn to write a Faith Page column for the *Mercury* coincides with February 14 which is—gasp—Valentine's Day.

Saint Valentine, I think, was the patron saint of greeting cards and chocolates who lived back in the glory days of romantic love. If I was to write a column for Valentine's Day about romantic love I would say that, ahhh, well, romantic love is, well, a mystery. Yes, that's it, a mystery...wrapped in an enigma. Now, I want you to talk among yourselves.

Yes, OK, I've failed you. This is not a column about Valentine's Day. I can offer little insight into the subtle nature of romantic love. However, I did run into something this week that I thought was "loving." It was a quotation, actually. It came from the great Greek philosopher, Socrates. As the story goes, Socrates is at home practicing his business of philosophizing when he's approached by a man who greatly admires him. The man considers himself to be an ordinary man of no great wealth or intellect. Somehow, in some way, he wants to be of service.

"I am a poor man," he said to Socrates. "I have nothing else, but I give you myself." Socrates looked into the man's eyes and said, "Do you not see that you are giving me the most precious thing of all?"

Socrates said it. I think Jesus would have said it. The most precious gift of all is the gift of self.

Let's take an example from daily life. There's little question that charitable organizations of all shapes and sizes need our financial donations to keep their heads above water and do their good work. But, financial support can be "easy" for the giver. It doesn't mean I "love" the organization or even know very much about it. Love only comes with the gift of self.

When I give my time to an organization; when I respect it; when my spirit lives there; that's when I love it. No organization I put my money into can survive without those who give themselves, day in and day out, to do its work. That's love. No effort to help others can survive long as a temporary, detached act of charity.

To give a little bit may accomplish a little bit. But to genuinely give oneself is the source of healing and wholeness. It's also the core of progress and accomplishment. To give oneself is the signal of a genuine love.

Giving oneself is a tricky business, of course. With due respect to Socrates, many of us have been burned by people and organizations who've allowed us to give and give until we're emotionally and spiritually dry. There are "takers" out there who are quite happy for us to "give until it hurts," and then some.

How do we know when giving ourselves is really about a healthy, wholesome, and healing love? My faith tells me that love is patient and kind; that it's unselfish and cares about the truth. My faith tells me that love is genuine when you give your heart to something and your heart is bigger because of it. Love is genuine when you give your strength and power to something and your spirit is stronger and more powerful because of it. Love is genuine when you give yourself and your "self" thrives because of it.

Valentine's Day is a great day to think and talk about love. Hopefully, not the only day, but a great day. I think the ancient encounter between the "ordinary man" and Socrates is going to stick in my mind for awhile.

"I'm a poor man," the average guy said. "I have nothing else, but I give you myself." And Socrates offered a message for the ages: "Do you not see that you are giving me the most precious thing of all?"

With thanks to Socrates, I wish you a happy Valentine's Day. The dog must have eaten the rest of my notes. Please, talk among yourselves.

A Time for Reflection:

Discuss the "Rich Young Man" of this week's scripture lesson. Do you feel sympathy for him? Anger? Do you think the key barriers to commitment are always money and possessions?

What is the action commitment (be as specific as you can) that you would like to make to God and your fellow human beings at this point in your life?

What are the things in your life that stand in the way of your making that commitment and living it out?

Describe the "space" your "self" occupies right now. Is it self-involved? Other - involved? Stuck in neutral? Stifled? Suffering from lack of exercise?

What does "genuine love" mean for you at this point in your life? How do you feel it? How do you exercise it on a day to day basis?

What will happen to God's world if the vast majority of the "rich" continue to stay self-involved?

A Time for Prayer:

Loving God, guide us to the place in our lives where we can genuinely trust in your love and bravely commit our best selves to the healing of a broken world. We confess to being caught up in the cynicism of the world. We are taught to horde the good and valuable things which surround us, to hold them tight so they can't be stolen from us. In our hording, in our fear, we've tied our spirits up in chains. Forgive us, we pray. Guide us to the healing humility which allows us to surrender those things which steal away our love, and which opens us to give ourselves freely to you. Amen.

A Time for Action:

The action you must take is challenging and life-changing. You must focus on the questions above with tremendous courage and intensity. Be totally honest with yourself. Prayerfully decide what your action commitment needs to be in the world today; what your best "self" longs to achieve. Then, one by one, define and break down the barriers that stand in the way of the person God is calling you to be.

Week 8: The Power of Inspiration

There is no more compelling power in the world today than the power of genuine inspiration. It moves us out of ourselves and beyond our fears. It gives us the courage to approach our most noble dreams and ask, "Why not?"

The Gospel of Matthew is pretty sparse in the details when it comes to tell the story of how Peter, Andrew, James, and John were called to be disciples. Jesus calls. They follow. Period. But, do you think these four fishermen, two sets of brothers, would simply drop their nets, leave their boats, and surrender their livelihoods if they hadn't been profoundly inspired by Jesus? We can only imagine the profound impact the person, the words, and the ministry of Jesus must have had on these men for them to make such a profound, life-changing commitment.

We don't step out of our comfort zone unless we're inspired to do so. We don't throw away the comfort of routine unless there's a new power working in our spirits. Peter, Andrew, James, and John followed Jesus because they were deeply inspired by his mission. They shared a compelling feeling that Jesus was a man who lived closer to God than anyone they'd ever known.

As he walked by the Sea of Galilee, he saw two brothers, Simon, who is called Peter, and Andrew his brother, casting a net into the sea—for they were fishermen. And he said to them, "Follow me, and I will make you fish for people." Immediately, they left their nets and followed him. As he went from there, he saw two other brothers, James son of Zebedee and his brother John, in the boat with their father Zebedee, mending their nets, and he called them. Immediately they left the boat and their father, and followed him. (Matthew 4: 18-22)

A Personal Journey:

I still have vivid memories of trudging up a very steep, very long hill to get to the Union Congregational Church in the little town of North Reading, Massachusetts. I was 12 years old and the memory doesn't have anything to do with Sunday morning services. Actually, the day I remember is Saturday.

Every Saturday morning for three months about 15 of us would climb the hill and converge on our church for a two-hour confirmation class with the Reverend Kenneth Boyle. Being 12 years old, I considered myself an expert on all subjects, even though I could barely spell most of them. So, as I entered confirmation class for the first time, I thought I could pretty much bluff my way through this whole religion "thing."

But, I didn't take the Reverend Boyle into account. Right from the start of the first class, he was a "presence." I don't mean he was an angry or frightening presence. He didn't scare us into submission. What he did was capture our imaginations.

He was so committed and so enthusiastic about his faith that we all got caught up in it. He was so knowledgeable, so eager, and so powerful a teacher that we just had to know more. He was fair to us and he challenged us to work and think. Of course, we couldn't put it into words at the time, but we knew that this man was genuine. He was a man of deep faith who really cared about the motley crew of pre-teens who showed up each Saturday morning for confirmation class.

It was at the Reverend Boyle's confirmation classes that I first remember feeling powerfully inspired. I remember how exciting it felt to think, dream, and reach higher than I'd ever imagined. Everything seemed possible because I believed it was possible. Reverend Boyle's God was becoming a powerful force in my own life.

It strikes me that the need for inspiration is a critical part of who we are as human beings. We *need* something to ignite us, something that causes us to think, dream, and reach higher than we ever imagined. It's how we progress; how we move our world towards more genuine, caring community.

The problem, of course, is that we don't all have jobs, tasks, or responsibilities that inspire us. For many of us, day to day life is pretty ordered and regular—even a little mundane. Our lives may not be bad but they keep us pinned down in the same set of rooms day after day. It's easy to get cynical or depressed in a world of "same old, same old."

But, particularly in a world like ours, where the focus is so often on war, terrorism, and weapons of mass destruction, we need to find inspiration. We need to find the people, hear the stories, and do the things that excite us to think, dream, and reach higher than we ever imagined. The people, stories, and "things to do" are out there for us. We may not have to go very far to find them.

Wouldn't it be great if we focused on inspirational stories with the same degree of intensity that we use to worry about war in Afghanistan and Iraq, or international terrorism? Wouldn't it be even greater if we *became* an inspirational story ourselves by thinking, dreaming, and reaching higher than we ever imagined?

As we've seen lately, the world regresses when it's afraid. It only advances when it's inspired.

A Time for Reflection:

Think of someone who has been an inspiration in your life. What was this person like? What were the qualities that you saw in this person? What did he/she do that inspired you?

If Jesus were to come to you, like he did to Peter, Andrew, James, and John, and say, "Follow me," what would you do? Do you think you could drop everything and become a disciple? Why or why not? What's the alternative?

What would life look like for you if you were to follow your most exciting dream and reach higher than you've ever reached before?

What kind of inspiration do you need to follow a cherished dream?

What qualities do you have right now that inspire others?

A Time for Prayer:

Gracious God, you are our power, our spirit, and our inspiration. Guide us to that place of courage where we can dream dreams and make them come to life. Guide us to reject despair and depression and turn our faces towards Jesus Christ as the beacon for our lives. In Christ, may we seek new pathways of service, hope, and healing. May the beacon of Christ one day fill us and surround us until we feel his powerful spirit lifting us higher than we ever imagined possible. Amen.

A Time for Action:

There is only one course of action. Remembering the inspiration of Christ and all the Christ-like people of your life, choose one of your most vital dreams and, as a person of faith and integrity, do everything that's fair and just to make that dream a reality.

Week 9: Finding Easter Spirit Down by the Creek

The scribes and Pharisees were two powerful sects in Jesus' day who figured that their tickets to heaven were already punched. They were prayerful and devout. They rigorously followed the religious laws, customs, and traditions of their day and considered themselves to be above reproach. But, much of faith for them was form over substance. They often failed to go deeper than the surface of their beliefs. They didn't allow their faith to take the critical leap towards justice and mercy; towards new understandings of life and hope. Their faith was stagnant and hypocritical— and Jesus called them on it!

"Woe to you, scribes and Pharisees, hypocrites! For you tithe mint, dill, and cummin, and have neglected the weightier matters of the law: justice and mercy and faith. It is these you ought to have practiced without neglecting the others. You blind guides! You strain out a gnat but swallow a camel!" (Matthew 23: 23-24)

A Personal Journey:
He was a terrible man. A ferocious man. Rumour was that if he caught tender ten-year-olds like us cutting through his yard, it would be THE END for us. He'd fry us in butter and eat us for his Sunday dinner.

His name was Wilbur and he was at least eight feet tall, covered in white hair, and ramrod straight. They said his face was horribly disfigured and his hands were like lethal weapons—blocks of concrete. That's what *they* said, anyway—my friends. No one had actually seen Wilbur close up, of course. No one dared look.

Wilbur's house, with its beautifully manicured lawn, was on the edge of a cool, dark swamp, which just added to the mystery and fear.

Unfortunately, you could cut through Wilbur's yard and save five minutes on your walk home from school. If you dared, that is. If you didn't care about being fried in butter. If you were brave enough to stare death in the face.

Naturally, my little pack of friends was constantly challenging one another to cut through Wilbur's yard. If you were one of the hangers-on, like me, you'd hear it all the time: "What's the matter? Are you a baby? Are you scared? C'mon man, show us what you've got!"

One Spring day, I showed them. Tired of being picked on, I suddenly began to sprint across Wilbur's yard. I could hear the cheers in the background at the same time that my legs began to weaken and wobble at the sheer immensity of this mistake.

And then I saw him. Wilbur. Standing by his shed, pitchfork in hand. "What are you doing?" he shouted. "I told you kids to stay out of my yard!" I put my head down and ran as fast as I could, praying that my legs would stay under me. I jumped the fence on the far side of the property, slipped, and did a face-plant in a large mud puddle. I could hear my friends' laughter back on the road.

When they caught up with me five minutes later, I told them that Wilbur was at least 12 feet tall, with sharp, pointed teeth, and a face so disfigured you couldn't tell where anything was. It was just what they wanted to hear and they spread the word.

The following summer, when my friend Peter and I were playing by the creek which bordered Wilbur's property, we suddenly felt this "presence" standing behind us. It was Wilbur. It had to be him. But, this wasn't the angry, disfigured, giant Wilbur who fried little children in butter and ate them for Sunday dinner. This was a quiet, gentle man. He looked like my grandfather, with close-cropped white hair and a rugged, deeply-lined face tinted red from too much time in the sun.

Wilbur talked to us about the little creek as if he loved every bend of it, every trickle of water. He told us about brook trout, frogs, salamanders, grasses, bushes, and trees. How they all depended on this little creek. Peter and I were mesmerized. We could feel his joy; his sense of wonder; an unbridled love for the natural world around him.

This was Wilbur. He wasn't at all the stereotype of evil we'd conjured up. He didn't personify everything to be feared and avoided in life. He was a man. A man who could love and feel with more intensity than Peter and I had ever experienced in our young lives. Wilbur was a man. I would never be afraid of him again. And, I would never cut through his yard again.

As we move slowly through Lent, towards Easter, this little story reminds me of what we have to gain by taking the journey. Without Easter, Wilbur remains an icon of fear. He is the grey eminence at the edge of the swamp, strange and terrifying. He is all we have stereotyped and demanded him to be. He is life without the sun, dangerous and untouchable. We have made him ugly and we will not allow him to feel pain, pity, or loneliness. Without Easter, Wilbur is an image, burnished in our minds by stories which could never be true. How much of life on this earth do we fear and push away, as if there was no Easter?

But, of course, there is Easter! Wilbur showed us Easter on that summer's day down by the creek. He showed us life can't be defeated by the grey fog of our own stereotypes. He showed us how a dead man, a man slaughtered by society's selfishness and fear, can be very much alive and vital. Wilbur taught us to be open to all the possibilities of life; to live on the joyful edge of surprise and wonder.

Wilbur died 35 years ago. I never thanked him for that Easter moment. I don't imagine he expected thanks or even suspected how powerfully God was working through him that day.

It's a little late, but thanks Wilbur—thanks for your spirit—thanks for showing us Easter.

A Time for Reflection:

How often in your life have form, stereotypes, fear, or public perception kept you from truly understanding another person or a set of events in your community or the world? Talk about those instances and how you felt.

What part do justice and mercy play in your religious beliefs?

If Wilbur reached out to you, would you be able to reach back? Would you be able to extend your hand first?

How hard or easy is it in your personal experience to find Easter in the day to day challenges and encounters of life; to find the places where life triumphs over death and to celebrate that victory? Try to name some instances and talk about the "victory." What kind of attitude must you have to find Easter in daily life?

Where is Christ in today's world? Does he still chastise the scribes and Pharisees?

A Time for Prayer:

Gracious God, help us to overcome the stereotypes that keep us from doing justice and sharing mercy with the stranger in our community. Help us to overcome the fear of difference that isolates us from our neighbour's wisdom. Loving God, give us the faith and strength to find Easter—to find life—even in those places where we're afraid and when we want to run away and hide. Your will be done. Amen.

A Time for Action:

Reach out to someone or some group who you've been afraid of, or anxious about, in the past. Find their life and their truth and share your own life and truth with them.

Week 10: What's Your Metaphor for Hope?

The Bible is filled with metaphors for hope. No matter how beaten and crushed people may be by their own shortcomings or by outside forces, there is always a sign of hope somewhere on the horizon. One of the most dramatic metaphors for hope in scripture is the story of Ezekiel and the valley of the dry bones. The great prophet envisions a huge valley filled with the bones of his divided and defeated nation. There is not a whiff of life or a scent of hope anywhere in this scene. Then God asks Ezekiel if these bones could possibly live again. The prophet has no answer except to say that such new life depends on God alone. And then the answer comes. God tells Ezekiel to prophesy to the bones, to the broken nation, telling them that God will breathe new life into them; that God will renew them and bring them from death and despair to life and hope. The people must listen and the people must have faith.

The hand of the Lord came upon me, and he brought me out by the spirit of the Lord and set me down in the middle of a valley; it was full of bones. He led me all around them; there were very many lying in the valley, and they were very dry. He said to me, "Mortal, can these bones live?" I answered, "O Lord God, you know." Then he said to me, "Prophesy to these bones, and say to them: O dry bones, hear the word of the Lord. Thus says the Lord God to these bones: I will cause breath to enter you, and you shall live; and you shall know that I am the Lord." (Ezekiel 37: 1-6)

A Personal Journey:

Did you ever wonder why we actually celebrate the dawn of a new year on January 1? Frankly, not being a winter person, I find it difficult to rejoice when the month of January arrives. You remember January don't you? Day after day of bone-chilling cold, broken occasionally by a horizontal snowstorm.

And, to be honest, I'm not enamoured with February either. It's just another January with a little "tease" thrown in. The second month of the year often lulls you with a pleasant little mild spell before it pummels you with bone-chilling cold, broken occasionally by a horizontal snowstorm. On February 2, of course, we get to celebrate Groundhog Day. As often as not, Wiarton Willie, in the good years when he's actually alive, emerges from his hole and sees his shadow. This is supposed to be bad news because it means we'll have another six weeks of winter. By my calculations, this means winter would be over in mid-March. Can anyone tell me why that's bad news? When was the last time any Canadian winter called it quits in mid-March?

Perhaps I digress a bit. But, I think you get my point. I simply can't find much to celebrate in a brand new year that starts on January 1.

My theory is that, in addition to being a good excuse for a party, we need to celebrate the new year because it gives us a sense of renewal and rejuvenation. Put the old to bed and bring on the new! It's a fresh year with fresh hope! Which is great, of course, but why do we have to start this new year off in the depths of January? Personally, if you want to talk about fresh hope, I'd rather celebrate the new year with a happy bash in March. Right about now.

It's not that March is a real gem of a month. Not by a long shot! But, here's the thing: March is the month that Spring training swings into high gear for major league baseball. Is there a better sign, signal, or metaphor for hope than Spring training? What's past is prologue. The boys of Summer are starting up again. Injuries and wounded egos have healed, and everything is fresh and new. Hope springs eternal, as they say. This is the year of the great breakthrough. This is the year that everything gets turned on its head. Dreams and visions come alive again like those baffling little flowers that push through rotting snow every Spring.

When I was young I was a reasonably good baseball player cruising the outfield for a reasonably good American university team. Each year we would go south to Florida to play a few games before the snow melted back home. One year we were invited over to "Tigertown" in central Florida to play a game against some of the Detroit Tigers' aspiring recruits. I don't remember much about the game (it was 35 years ago), but I'll never forget the energy of the place. Young people putting on the uniform and living the dream. Nothing could stop them; they were headed to the major leagues. This was their chance and they were going to give it everything they had. Hope seemed to bathe and invigorate this little speck of earth and even though I knew 99 percent of these kids would never see a day in the majors, I still admired them for trying...for believing.

I suspect that every one of us has a metaphor for hope. When we're ready for the metaphor, that's probably when the new year starts. That's when renewal and rejuvenation happens; when injuries and wounded egos are healed and everything is fresh and new.

I think the new year can start anytime we want it to start. It starts when our own metaphor for hope takes hold of us; when we know we're headed to the major leagues and nothing is going to stop us.

I'm not quite ready to celebrate the new year in January or February with my head down and my shoulders folded in against the cold and snow. But, March—that's when my metaphor kicks in again; that's when I can celebrate a new year filled with hope. That's when Spring training is in high gear.

So now I can rightfully say Happy New Year. And one final wish. May your own metaphors for hope—for new life—always stay strong and healthy for you.

A Time for Reflection:

Name the things that are hurting your spirit right now; the things that drag you down, that put you in "the valley of dry bones."

Take a moment to listen. What is God saying to you right now about your spirit?

Where do you find renewal and rejuvenation in your life? Name/make a list of the ways in which God breathes life into the dry bones of your spirit when you're feeling down.

What's your greatest metaphor for hope in this world? Why does it mean so much to you?

What actions do you need to take in your day to day life that show how important your "greatest metaphor for hope" is to you?

A Time for Prayer:

Gracious God, these bones sometimes get very dry. There are times when the losses of our lives far outweigh the gains and our spirits are very low. Open us to the life-giving breath of your spirit. Open us to finding and living out the hope which lives inside us. Give us the courage to overcome the anger and self-pity that makes our bones so dry and to rise up once again to be all you've gifted us to be and to achieve all you've gifted us to achieve. Amen.

A Time for Action:

What's the dream that's buried in the dry bones of your spirit; the dream you're aching to realize if you could only be filled with hope once again? Talk about your dream with a trusted friend, relative, or mentor so that you know clearly what it is and what it entails. God has lifted your spirit and given you new hope and new life. If your dream is true at its core, now is the time to reach for it.

Week 11: How Rich Do You Want to Be?

Over the years, people have spent their time counting the number of times the Bible mentions everything from "Amen" to "Zechariah". One thing the zealous counters have discovered is that a primary topic of conversation, particularly in the New Testament, is money and wealth. The whole concept of wealth is raised repeatedly in scripture because our relationship to our possessions can either open us up to the wonders of God's kingdom or seal us off as if we lived in a different, much more hostile dimension.

The Bible is constantly talking to us about material wealth and abundance and warning us to be thoroughly conscious of their power. It's says, essentially, that true abundance can never be found in a bank vault. It can only be found in the human spirit, and it only has value when it's shared with others. What's not dedicated to God's kingdom becomes the twine that ties us up in knots.

No good tree bears bad fruit, nor again does a bad tree bear good fruit; for each tree is known by its own fruit. Figs are not gathered from thorns, nor are grapes picked from a bramble bush. The good person out of the good treasure of the heart produces good, and the evil person out of evil treasure produces evil; for it is out of the abundance of the heart that the mouth speaks.
(Luke 6: 43-45)

A Personal Journey:

My favourite magazine puts out a special issue each year that advises readers about how to get richer. They do a masterful job of describing the mutual fund marketplace, real estate opportunities, stocks, bonds, and more recondite money-makers like exchange traded funds, income trusts, and hedge funds. It's great background for those who are serious about growing their money.

Of course, the operative word in all this information is "richer." There's an assumption that the reader already has money and just needs a few solid options for getting richer. As a freelance writer, I have to say that I'm not absorbed with the notion of increasing my vast fortune. My internal drama has more to do with making ends meet. If my favourite magazine should ever come out with a special issue on "Clinging to Solvency", I'll read it from cover to cover.

I don't think it's sour grapes or wishful thinking to believe that there are other ways to get richer than playing the financial markets. And, I don't think my favourite magazine would disagree with me.

For example, while accruing more money can be fun, studies consistently show that the happiest, most contented people are those who know how to give it away. Newfoundlanders are among the best per capita givers to charity in Canada and there is arguably no group in this country who have a stronger, more positive sense of who they are as a people. Those who have the heart for giving to others, whether it's their money or their time, are very rich. And the more they exercise that "heart" the richer they'll be.

In his wonderful book, *Time Zones*, journalist Joe Schlesinger says people can turn the world into a living hell when they lose their sense of "common decency." Without understanding and respect for the culture, religion, and social values of others; without a holy regard for their dreams and visions, the world is a brutal place. One critical way to get richer is to deepen our sense of common decency.

One of my favourite little sayings has to do with carrying a grudge. Like most people, I've been known to carry them, so this little aphorism has deep meaning for me. "To carry resentment in your heart," the saying goes, "is to take poison and expect someone else to die." Forgiveness helps to purge life of the toxins that make it painful and unhealthy. Forgiveness helps to expel the anger that rivets us in place. Our lives will not become richer if we can't forgive others—if we can't forgive ourselves—for the real or imagined transgressions that serve to consume and poison our thoughts.

My trusty dictionary defines "hope" as "expectation and desire combined." This is the Canadian Oxford Dictionary's way of saying that, if we fail to carry a shining, achievable vision into the future, we're just going to be lost in the darkness. Hope comes in many sizes, of course. It can be the weak, virtually inaudible voice that keeps us putting one foot in front of the other, day in and day out. Or, it can be a powerful, consuming voice that gives us strength, direction, and joy—a genuine belief that what we expect and what we desire can actually happen. Those who find great hope will become richer.

Ministers and counselors often find themselves working with people who are struggling to find a "purpose" for their lives. These folks often can't name a single life-sustaining reason to get out of bed in the morning. They can't connect with any sense of hope. And, hope, you might say, is the gateway to purpose. People who are rich in hope are also rich in the spirit and the door is open to be rich in purpose. They'll find their life purpose in relationships with family and friends, in their work, in volunteering, in civic action, in sports, in arts and culture, or in a thousand different things. Those who deepen and expand their sense of purpose will become richer.

It would be wonderful if we could all increase our wealth every day and every year. But, first we might want to be clear in our own hearts and minds what constitutes genuine wealth in this world.

A Time for Reflection:

In what specific ways does material wealth interfere with your spiritual wealth today?

How do you feel when the two forms of "richness," material and spiritual, actually collide and you must choose one over the other? Do they need to collide?

Take a litmus test for your spiritual wealth. How do you feel about yourself as a giver? As a person who exercises common decency? As a person who forgives? As a person of hope? As a person of purpose?

If your spiritual wealth isn't where you want it to be, what changes do you need to make in order to get there?

Go back to the scripture passage for today and read it again. What does it mean to live in a world where both good and bad fruit can be found in abundance? How will you know which way to turn for mentors; for support in your life journey?

A Time for Prayer:

Loving God, open us to the abundance of your blessed kingdom. Guide us to keep our possessions in their proper place and strive for the good treasures of the heart which help to bring the transforming power of your love to a broken world. Make us vessels, Lord, and fill us with the spirit of giving, with common decency, with forgiveness, with hope, and with purpose. All that we are, all that we have, all that we can be, is by your grace and from your bounty, Lord. Amen.

A Time for Action:

Think about your world right now. Take one step for a richer spiritual life. Perhaps you need to explore your own generosity. Make that gift of time and/or money that has been weighing on your mind. Perhaps you need to take a new step in connecting with people of other faiths and cultures, to understand what has made you fearful or uncomfortable. Perhaps you need to forgive someone and begin to forge a healthier relationship. Above all, take one step for a richer spiritual life and take it now. You may find that it's the first step of a long, fruitful journey.

Week 12: Do Faith and Intellect Need to be at Odds?

One of the most profound failings of the terminally religious Christian is that we actually think we know what we know. We subscribe to a body of "knowledge" that was not set out by independent historians, but by committed partisans who wanted the world to believe in Jesus Christ and his life-giving power. What we know is only what we choose to believe. What we believe is what gives us the strength to meet our challenges, to grow as individuals, and to live an abundant life. But we don't really know what we know.

The Apostle Paul cautions us against assuming that our "truth" is the only truth when he writes, "For now we see in a mirror, dimly..." The fact is, there's much more to explore in our faith. We have not even begun, with loving candor, to explore the boundaries of our beliefs. Christianity is an open book, not a closed one. It's exciting when people challenge the boundaries and start to push at them and expand them. It's a sign that our faith is alive and vibrant in today's world.

When I was a child, I spoke like a child, I thought like a child, I reasoned like a child; when I became an adult, I put an end to childish ways. For now we see in a mirror, dimly, but then we will see face to face. Now I know only in part; then I will know fully, even as I have been fully known. And now faith, hope, and love abide, these three; and the greatest of these is love. (1 Corinthians 13: 11-13)

A Personal Journey:

Many Christians today, to be honest, have quite a struggle taking the faith literally. It's a very uncomfortable stretch for the modern person to suspend their understandings of science and the physical world to accept a human Jesus who could walk on water; or change water into wine; or feed 5,000 people with five loaves of bread and two fish. It's even more uncomfortable to think of a human Jesus resuscitating the dead Lazarus; or even being physically resuscitated himself as the Easter story unfolds.

I, of course, grew up in the arms of Mother Church. I became a card-carrying Christian at a very young age. If I'd been born in Iran, I might well be following a different religion right now. For many of us, we're born into our faith and grow up surrounded with its doctrines. Sometimes, as we mature, those doctrines can be quite a challenge. I grew up being educated about the physical properties and realities of the natural world in public school and being ordered to deny all those properties and realities in my faith. There was only one way to take the Christian faith back then—literally. The intellect needed to take the day off on Sunday. The laws of nature, apparently, could be defied on that day.

But is it really necessary to either take religious faith literally or just walk away? Do we need to either suspend our intellect or abandon our faith? A few years ago, Tom Harpur, one of Canada's finest writers on contemporary religion, wrote a challenging, insightful book entitled *The Pagan Christ*. In the book, Harpur says it's long past time to reclaim the spiritual, symbolic purpose of our religious stories. What's critical are the "eternal myths," alive in the dramatic stories of all religions, which help us understand the nature of the "divine."

Harpur's point is that the gospel story isn't to be taken literally so much as it's to be mined for eternal truths about humanity and divinity. Extreme literalism has historically led to arrogance, division, and sectarian violence among those who purport to be seeking the same eternal truths. It's not the literal story that matters, he says. That's only a delivery system. It's the spiritual meaning imbued in the story that's important and unifying.

So, during the lead-up to Easter, what if we boldly and courageously decided not to take the Easter story literally? Would such a stance signal the end of Christianity? It might be bad news for Mel Gibson's movie-making, but it certainly doesn't mean the demise of the faith. In fact, it might give us a chance to focus on Easter's critical meaning to us as spiritual beings.

In John 1:5 it says, "The light shines in the darkness, and the darkness did not overcome it." Isn't that the profound spiritual meaning of Easter? The divine spiritual light that lives within each one of us can be jostled, dimmed, ignored, and threatened by ourselves and by the world around us but it is not going to be extinguished. The divine spirit, or "the Christ within" in Christian terms, is the power of life over death in the very real decisions, crises, and challenges of everyday life. Easter is the radical story of what it means to have the eternal, liberating, empowering gift of "the Christ within." It mirrors other stories from other faiths that help us understand the power of the divine spirit to transform our lives and the life of the world. Even though our intellect may compel us to understand the Easter story as "eternal myth," it is no less life-giving and faith-inspiring than any other form of interpretation.

Of course, we'll each experience the Easter story in our own way. Some of us will struggle with literalism, others will embrace it. Ultimately, what's important is that the message of Easter be life-giving and unifying; that the divine spiritual light continues to shine in our world, granting us new levels of wisdom.

A Time for Reflection:

If you were to make the intellectual decision that the "miracle stories" of the Bible, including the resurrection of Christ, were not literally true events, would that mean the end of faith for you? Why or why not?

What do you think are some of the "eternal myths" which are alive in all religions?

What would be the implications for your religious faith if you had been born and raised in Iran? How would that impact your understanding of faith?

As we engage the Lent-Easter season what do you see as Easter's critical meaning to us as spiritual beings?

What does it mean to a Christian in daily life to feel "the Christ within?" Can you name examples where "the Christ within" has influenced you?

We don't really know what we know. Do you find this statement worrisome or liberating for your faith? What is the role in life for a people who only "see in a mirror, dimly?"

A Time for Prayer:

Gracious God, open us to the power of the intellect. Help us to see knowledge and inquiry as a great gift, not a stumbling block to faith. Stretch us God. Push the boundaries of our faith with the challenges of a searching, diligent, and honest questioning. Loving God, we often cannot accept the dimness of our sight. We know what we know. We're not open to a new world of possibilities which would expand our faith and deepen our love. Help us, God, to find the confidence of our faith. Amen.

A Time for Action:

Read a book, attend a lecture, take a course, see a movie, engage in a discussion, or go to a worship that stretches the boundaries of your faith. Decide if this "stretching" serves to animate "the Christ within" or whether it has some other effect. If you are "stretched" in a positive way, define and act upon a new "mission" which is now within your boundaries.

Week 13: Lisa's Lesson About Humanity

Charity can be a pretty "sketchy" concept sometimes. The reasons we decide to support charitable causes and organizations are extraordinarily diverse and occasionally rather muddy. We give to a health charity because a particular illness may have affected us or our extended family at some point. We give to the poor because it's our duty to give. We have so much and they have so little. We give to a global cause because we respect the celebrity asking for the donation. We give to disaster relief because the pictures we see are so heart-rending. How can we not give?

The bottom line is that it feels noble to give. The healthy, wealthy, and successful have an obligation to give to their opposite numbers "out there"—whoever they may be. After all, where would those people be without our generous acts of charity?

Charity becomes sketchy when it divides the world into winners and losers; when the donor lacks any real connection to the person being helped, and doesn't see the need for one. The question remains, how do we frame our generosity in ways which honour the dignity and humanity of both giver and receiver?

As it is, there are many members, yet one body. The eye cannot say to the hand, "I have no need of you," nor again the head to the feet, "I have no need of you." On the contrary, the members of the body that seem to be weaker are indispensable, and

*those members of the body we think less
honourable we clothe with greater honour, and our
less respectable members are treated with greater
respect...*
(1 Corinthians 12: 20-23)

A Personal Journey:

A few years ago, I was a senior fundraiser for The
United Church of Canada's national mission fund.

One of the little perks of my job back then was the
occasional trip to gather stories about the good work
our $30 million fund was doing in the world. In the fall
of 1999, I traveled to Vancouver to visit one of the
United Church's oldest urban missions, First United
Church. On the downtown eastside of the city, First
United is located right in the middle of what is often
called the roughest, poorest, most drug-ravaged
neighbourhood in Canada.

The mission staff gave me a top-to-bottom tour of
their crowded facility and I was eventually deposited
on the edges of a weekly fellowship group that
provided a program and a lunch to people from the
neighbourhood. The staff person introduced me.
"This is Dean Salter," he said. "You'd better be nice to
him. He provides the money that keeps this program
going."

All eyes turned towards me. I wanted to say, 'Look
folks, I help raise it, I have no say where it goes.' But,
I just smiled and let the moment pass. So they think
I'm a big shot—so what?

Suddenly, a craggy, forty-something woman in a
wheelchair spun towards me. She was about 10 feet
away and she gave me a hard, angry stare that made
me glance over my shoulder at the nearest exit. Later,
I discovered that her name was Lisa and she'd been
through enough pain, disaster, and death for three

lifetimes. Right now, she was focusing all her attention on me.

"You'd better not cut us off, buddy," she said, "or I'll run you over with my wheelchair."

I backed away a few feet and figured the next thing I said had better be the right thing. But, all I could say was, "I hear you." She spun the wheelchair back around and rejoined the group.

I've often thought about that little incident. Initially, I thought, 'Well, she's got a lot of nerve. We're providing a bunch of cash to this place and she's ready to run me over at a moment's notice.' Over time, I've thought differently.

I think Lisa was teaching me about life in community. In her own rough and ready way, she was making a vital statement. She was saying that this place and this time were her joy. This is where she got her personal power; this is where she felt her human dignity.

If I thought this was about a few dollars in the offering plate—an arms-length act of charity—I was wrong. This was about her life, her power, and her dignity. Every human being should crave nothing less for every other human being than a life that's rich in personal power and dignity. That's not charity, Lisa was telling me. You don't give that to me like you're tossing away a toonie. We work together so every person can have it. I have a right to control my life and to live with dignity. We have a responsibility to one another to make that happen, not just for me, but for everybody.

Lisa wasn't thankful for the money we were putting into her favourite program. She didn't need to be. She, particularly, wasn't thankful for the kind of giving that divides the community between the "noble" giver and the "grateful" recipient. She was more concerned about a single, unified "community of people" totally intertwined with one another, a community where each is concerned about the other's life, power, and human dignity. In this community, giving is not throwing a few dollars at the disadvantaged. It's a commitment to life, and we have a right to expect it of one another.

So, Lisa, you scared me to death back in the fall of 1999. But, you also taught me something. It's not about charity. It's about the common linkages of all humanity—all of life. If you're diminished, so am I. If your community is broken, so is mine.

A Time for Reflection:

How do you decide whether or not to make a charitable donation? What parameters do you use? How much do you know about the organization and the people you're "supporting?" How much should you know?

How does the act of charitable giving make you feel? Why do you feel that way?

How does it make you feel when those who benefit from charitable giving don't seem very thankful or respectful towards the givers? Why do you feel that way?

In your own words, what would you say was Lisa's lesson about humanity? How do you feel about that lesson?

In your view, what needs to change in our world for people to genuinely believe that "there are many members, yet one body?"

A Time for Prayer:

Loving God, give us strength, courage, and hearts of generosity to be forces for unity rather than division in this world. Where the spirit of community is broken help us to feel that, wherever it might be, it's still *our* community. Its health is our health. Its success is our success. Where life is diminished by greed, intolerance, and the willful hatred that seeks to divide people into "winners" and "losers," guide us Lord to be instruments of peace and healing. May we learn to be strong links in the circle of life. Amen.

A Time for Action:

Make a conscious and thorough effort to connect with and learn about a charitable organization or cause to which you feel drawn. Who are the people being served? What have their lives been like? Why do they need support right now? What social, economic, and political forces affect their lives? Get to know those being helped, along with the staff and volunteers who work with them. Make a conscious decision about how you should use your time and financial resources to strengthen the community in which you live.

Week 14: Finding the Heart of God

In many ways, Palm Sunday, the day we mark Jesus' triumphant entry into Jerusalem, is the beginning of the end for Jesus. After this very public spectacle, staged to fulfill the biblical prophecy that the true king will come riding into Jerusalem on a donkey, events quickly spiral towards the crucifixion. No one understands this spiral of death more clearly than Jesus himself. It's not surprising that, as he comes close to the city, Jesus begins to weep. Is it possible that he's crying for all of us? Is it possible he's speaking to all of us when he says, "If you, even you, had only recognized on this day the things that make for peace! But now they are hidden from your eyes." Palm Sunday is the beginning of a tragedy in which we still haven't discovered the resurrection of peace.

As he rode along people kept spreading their cloaks on the road. As he was now approaching the path down from the Mount of Olives, the whole multitude of the disciples began to praise God joyfully with a loud voice for all the deeds of power that they had seen, saying, "Blessed is the king who comes in the name of the Lord! Peace in heaven, and glory in the highest heaven." Some of the Pharisees in the crowd said to him, "Teacher, order your disciples to stop." He answered, "I tell you, if these were silent, the stones would shout out." (Luke 19: 36-40)

A Personal Journey:

This weekend, Christians around the world will celebrate Palm Sunday in worship. Palm fronds will be waved by fresh-faced children as they march around the sanctuary and hallelujahs will echo to the rafters of churches near and far. And all the people will shout, "Blessed is the king who comes in the name of the Lord!"—or something like that.

In our usually quiet churches, the spectacle of Palm Sunday is a pleasant change. Who wouldn't welcome the chance to raise a ruckus? Who wouldn't welcome the chance to celebrate a triumphant moment in the faith?

When you read the Gospels, you wonder if people actually got a little too hyped up with the moment. "Blessed is the king...," Jesus' followers called out as if this royal figure on the donkey was about to kick the Roman occupiers out of town and establish a just new order within the next few days.

Expectations were high. You have to wonder, after all that Jesus said and did to help his followers understand the Kingdom of God, if they still dreamed of a political heavyweight who could free Israel from its oppressor. Old concepts of power and victory don't die easily.

Palm Sunday is exciting only as we understand that Jesus was ringing in a new kind of kingdom. Palm Sunday is meaningful when we wave the palms to celebrate a new kingdom where the first will be last and the last first; when we wave the palms to celebrate our ability to love our neighbour as ourselves; when we wave the palms to celebrate a love that gives freely and a peace that's centred in the heart of God.

Palm Sunday is an empty pleasure if it's all about winners and losers, victory and defeat. If it plays into the world as we know it, it has little meaning. If it celebrates a new "way," a radical new kingdom of thought and actions, it means everything.

What's it like, this new kingdom which we celebrate on Palm Sunday? A few days ago, I looked out my back window and saw a quiet, gentle, unspectacular snapshot of this new world. On the main road behind our house an elderly man was hunched over a wheelchair pushing an elderly woman up a long, steady grade on the sidewalk towards a large plaza about a kilometre away. It wasn't an easy task but the man was puffing along at a steady pace.

As they traveled by, I could feel a communion between them. There was something in the way they were talking and looking at one another that said, 'This is the way we love one another. This is the way we give from the heart and express our love.'

For the man, there was no power or prestige to be gained. There was no victory to be won. It was a simple act of giving, of expending his power and energy so his partner could enjoy the beauty of the day and do the things she needed to do at the plaza.

For the woman, it was an act of courage and trust— a giving of herself. She was saying to her partner, I love you and I trust you enough to make this journey with you. I'll show my disability to the world because you know that I'm strong. For this couple, the act of giving was their communion with one another.

The new kingdom that we celebrate on Palm Sunday is made of such things. The fabric of this kingdom is woven by those who don't live their lives in the hungry pursuit of money, power, and prestige but, rather, dedicate themselves to finding the heart of God in their daily lives.

When we wave the palm fronds on Palm Sunday we are honouring a new kind of "kingdom" where the first shall be last and the last first; where we can find it within ourselves to love our neighbours as we love ourselves; where love is self-giving and peace comes from the heart of God.

We aren't celebrating a final victory over the devils that torment us. We're celebrating a Great Vision and a Great Hope that plays itself out every day that someone lays down their palm frond and says, "I want to live in this radical new kingdom."

A Time for Reflection:

Think about/discuss what Palm Sunday has meant to you over the years from childhood to adulthood. What's the "feeling" of Palm Sunday for you?

This week's introduction concludes by saying, "Palm Sunday is the beginning of a tragedy in which we still haven't discovered the resurrection of peace." What does this statement mean for you and how do you feel about it? Do you think it's accurate? What impact does it have on your celebration of Palm Sunday?

Where do you see the "winners and losers" attitude active in the world today? How does it impact you and how do you feel about it? What impact does it have on the wider world?

What does the image of one person pushing another uphill on a wheelchair have to do with Palm Sunday? What do you see as the key message of the story which serves to connect the two?

If the things that make for peace weren't hidden from our eyes, what do you think we'd see?

A Time for Prayer:

Gracious God, on this Palm Sunday guide us to feel the tears of Christ in our own eyes. Help us to peel away the anger, suspicion, and mistrust that cloud our vision. Guide us to the peace which opens up a new world of possibilities for our lives. Loving God, we want to live in your radical new kingdom. Help us to let go of everything that ties us up and holds us back from taking the first steps of our journey. Amen.

A Time for Action:

So much of the world of work and play is predicated on the "need" to celebrate the "winners" and scorn/ridicule/ignore/pity the "losers." What can you do in your world of work or play this week that makes a clear statement you don't believe in a world divided between winners and losers? Is there someone or some group you want to reach out to? How will you "lay down your palm branch" and join the radical new kingdom?

Week 15: A Time to Celebrate Hope and Optimism

There is no more powerful and significant event in the life of Christianity than the resurrection of Jesus Christ. Whether we choose to believe in a physical or a spiritual resurrection, the meaning of this wonderful event remains the same. If the crucifixion of Christ on Good Friday represents the darkest and most forsaken moment of our human experience, the resurrection represents the fact that, even in our darkest, bleakest moments, hope has not left the world.

The resurrection tells us that life is a much more powerful and potent force than death. In every loss, there is the potential for victory. In every death there is the promise that life is not defeated. There is the assurance that God is not the God of scarcity but unquestionably the God of abundant life. The resurrection symbolizes hope—the hope that God is present for us, turning the "death" in our lives into renewal and vitality.

His appearance was like lightning and his clothing white as snow. For fear of him the guards shook and became like dead men. But the angel said to the women, "Do not be afraid; I know that you are looking for Jesus who was crucified. He is not here; for he has been raised, as he said. Come, see the place where he lay. Then go quickly and tell his disciples, 'He has been raised from the dead, and indeed he is going ahead of you to Galilee; there you will see him.' This is my message for you." So they left the tomb quickly with fear and great joy, and ran to tell his disciples. Suddenly Jesus met them and said, "Greetings!" And they came to him, took hold of his feet, and worshipped him. Then Jesus said to them, "Do not be afraid; go and tell my brothers to go to Galilee; there they will see me." (Matthew 28: 3-10)

A Personal Journey:

There's a story that's been around for quite a while about a fictional village nestled on the banks of a large river.

One day, the villagers noticed two people in the water being swept downstream. Courageously, a few of the villagers leaped into the water and saved them. The next day, there were four people being swept downstream. Again, the villagers leaped into the water and saved the waterlogged victims.

Every day, people were coming down the river, in greater and greater numbers. A lifesaving station was built on shore. People were trained in the latest lifesaving techniques. Soon, another station was built and then another. Still, people were being swept down the river, in greater and greater numbers.

Pretty soon, the little village didn't have much time to do anything else but pull people out of the river.

Finally, the village leaders gathered.

"We can't go on like this," said one. "There are too many people in the water and too few of us. What are we going to do?"

Then, the wisest person in the village spoke up. She said, "We must do all that we can here. But we must also travel as far as necessary up the river to find out why so many people have been swept into the water, and then do something about it."

Over the years, I've been privileged to meet and work with hundreds of people committed to providing emergency food, shelter, and other services for those pushed to the margins of our society. They work hard and they care deeply. Most are volunteers, motivated by their faith or their humanism. They do great work.

But, most of these men and women are convinced that the charitable deed isn't enough. Charity is necessary, even critical, in order to sustain people. But, it's not enough. They don't want to focus all their energy on pulling people out of the water. They want to travel as far as they can upstream to find out why so many people are in the water.

Why are so many people in food lines? Why can't they buy the food they need? Why are so many people homeless or struggling along in substandard housing? Why do they need castoff clothing? Why aren't there enough jobs to go around? What's going on up the river and how can we change it?

For Christians, Easter week is the holiest week of our faith. Easter is about many things, but, critically, it's about two things: transformation and renewal. Easter week closes with profound hope and optimism for the future. Life is victorious over death. It's a time for searching up the river and believing things can change.

The whole faith community knows very well that we can't go up the river alone. The only way to deal with the issues of poverty and deprivation in our society is through partnership. All our communities—religious, academic, business, charitable, and governmental— have to go up the river together, with the strong leadership of our elected officials, if transformation and renewal are going to happen. If any one group opts out we're all in trouble.

The wise woman of the village has issued a challenge to us all: "Travel together up the river to see what's causing the problems and then do something about it."

As Christians, our response to her challenge defines whether we truly believe in transformation and renewal; whether we can truly call ourselves an Easter people.

A Time for Reflection:

Do you think it's easy to go up the river? What stands in the way of making the trip?

What do you think you'd find up the river that creates such dysfunction and pain for so many?

Have you ever been washed down the river yourself? Describe a moment of darkness and "death" in your life. What was your resurrection? How did you come to experience new life?

What do you have difficulty believing when it comes to Easter Week and Easter? How do these questions impact your faith?

What do you firmly believe when it comes to Easter Week and Easter? How do your beliefs bring you hope in day to day living?

Describe what you feel it means in practical terms to live as part of the "Easter People."

A Time for Prayer:

God of resurrection and new life, scrape away the stale layers of doctrine and ritual that keep me from experiencing the true and vital power of Easter. Open me to naming the death and darkness that pin the corners of my days and take away the breath of my spirit. Open my eyes and my heart to new life in Jesus Christ. Help me to let the pain slip away and live freely in your grace. Help me to live with the sure knowledge that, in Christ, life will always have its victory over death. We praise your holy name. Amen.

A Time for Action:

Identify one place in your community where you see "death" at work. Christ is life. How can you "be Christ" to that situation you see? If there is no partnership to join, develop a strategy, engage partners, and take action yourself. Easter is about bringing life to a world pre-occupied with death. It's about going up the river and making a difference in Christ's name.

Week 16: The Radical Nature of Hope

The disciple Thomas, saddled for all eternity with the unfortunate nickname "Doubting Thomas," should really be cut some slack. After all, isn't he just a sharp, biting metaphor for all of us "rational" beings? He's no different than any of us, really. If you want me to believe something, then show me some absolute, concrete proof. I want to see the nail marks on Jesus' hands. I want to touch the scarred flesh of his side before I'll believe anything. I want proof that Jesus lives. I want facts and evidence that are incontrovertible by the rational human mind.

There's a strong part of us that wants to throw over faith, hope, and spirituality in favour of cold hard facts and empirical evidence. But, Jesus says, "Have you believed because you have seen me? Blessed are those who have not seen and yet have come to believe." Ultimately, how can humanity soar to new levels without the engine of hope? How do we grow without faith? How do we change cold, hard facts, and turn death into life, without spirit? (EDITOR'S NOTE: You'll find another take on "Doubting Thomas" and the value of having questions and feeling doubts when you get to week 43.)

But Thomas (who was called the Twin), one of the twelve, was not with them when Jesus came. So the other disciples told him, "We have seen the Lord." But he said to them, "Unless I see the mark of the

*nails in his hands, and put my finger in the mark of
the nails and my hand in his side, I will not believe."*

*A week later his disciples were again in the
house, and Thomas was with them. Although the
doors were shut, Jesus came and stood among
them and said, "Peace be with you." Then he said to
Thomas, "Put your finger here and see my hands.
Reach out your hand and put it in my side. Do not
doubt but believe." Thomas answered him, "My Lord
and my God!" Jesus said to him, "Have you believed
because you have seen me? Blessed are those who
have not seen and yet have come to believe."* (John
20: 24-29)

A Personal Journey:

Can anything good come out of a university whose
favourite party song starts out, "Drink a highball at
nightfall, be good fellows while ye may...?"

It seems doubtful. And, yet, I'm almost certain that
the University of Pennsylvania is considered one of the
better universities in the United States—purveyors of
fine education, if not fine party songs. This school in
the heart of Philadelphia is my alma mater. This was
the school I attended from 1967 to 1971. After the
passage of over 37 years, I must confess that my
academic retention is a little spotty. Very spotty, in
fact. The truth is, I can't remember one single
academic gem from those four years.

What I do remember is the day Phillip Berrigan came
to our campus.

Phillip Berrigan and his brother, Daniel, were
famous for their anti-war activism during the Vietnam
War. Phillip and Daniel, both Catholic priests, were
often on the front lines of massive protests. They were
the voices behind the bullhorns and their names had
become associated with radical anti-war activities. To

say the least, they were closely watched by "the powers that be."

Sitting with about 50 other sympathetic students crowded into a classroom, I listened to Berrigan's powerful anti-war rhetoric. A burning question came into my mind (not a common occurrence, believe me!). I asked him, knowing his reputation as a radical activist, "What's the most radical thing you can do today?"

He never missed a beat. His answer was something that caught me off guard, something that I've never forgotten. He said, "The most radical thing you can do today is to have hope."

I expected him to issue a call to the barricades. I expected a call to storm the citadels of power. But, for him, the most radical thing you can do as a human being is to have hope. I expected bombast and he gave me faith.

I've often thought of Berrigan's radical answer when reading the daily newspaper or watching the evening newscasts. Day after day, there are appalling stories coming out of the Middle East. Death and destruction are graphically laid out before our eyes. Historic enmities are overlaid with modern hatreds and there seems to be no end in sight.

In Africa, many nations live under crushing debt loads that make it almost impossible to meet health care and education needs. And the spectre of AIDS grows bigger and bolder each year.

Globally, civil wars and conflicts defeat all efforts at progress. Close to home, food banks are overwhelmed as more and more people cross below the poverty line. It's enough to make you throw your hands up in despair. Too many problems!

That's why the most radical thing you can do today is to have hope.

Berrigan was right. Hope is defiant, angry, and active. It refuses to give up. It motivates when there seems to be no logical reason for motivation. Hope looks at the world and says, "I know how things are...but I also believe this is how things can be." In a world that's becoming increasingly cynical, hope is as radical as it gets.

When I first heard Phillip Berrigan's answer to my question, I remember feeling an initial whiff of disappointment. I ask for "radical" and he gives me "hope!" But, of course, it was the only *real* answer and he reached deeply into his personal faith to give it.

A Time for Reflection:

Discuss the disciple Thomas. How do you feel about his doubts? Would you have them yourself? How is he a metaphor for the world we live in today?

Why do you think Phillip Berrigan said, "The most radical thing you can do today is to have hope?" Think about what that means for you, for your nation, and for your world.

If the most radical thing you can do is to have hope, is it necessary to go to the barricades for what you believe? What does hope actually mean for day to day living?

What sustains your hope when you see hunger, homelessness, war, upheaval, and disease in the world?

What needs to change in your life for you to live as a person of hope, as someone who believes in the victory of life over death in the "real" world?

What do you take from the fact "Doubting Thomas" remained a faithful disciple for his entire life?

A Time for Prayer:

Gracious God, thank you for holding me in your heart despite my doubts and denials. Thank you for accepting me when I stubbornly refuse to accept you.

Your grace waits like an unopened present, ready to show me a future where hope outshines despair and life is always victorious over death. Thank you for letting me touch your wounds. Thank you for loving me anyway and showing me the ways of faith. Thank you for inviting me into the future. Amen.

A Time for Action:

Go to the barricades for a cause in which you truly believe; a cause in which you see the face of God. Live your life as one who believes in the radical power of hope.

91

Week 17: The Amazing Race

Sometimes life can seem very much like one long, arduous race. As youth, we race to "succeed" in school, make some pocket money, and do the necessary things to fit in socially. As adults, we charge around trying to meet work, home, and volunteer commitments. The house needs to be cleaned and the kids need to be driven to their after school activities. Even recreation takes time and energy to plot and plan. Having fun can entail a supreme effort. And then there's the cottage to look after and, perhaps, extended family to include and support. There are times when the race is "amazing," but not in a good way.

The Apostle Paul occasionally liked to use sports metaphors to encourage the faithful. He would encourage people to run the race courageously and keep the ultimate goal in front of them. For him, the race wasn't a negative thing. Paul believed that if God was both the journey and the goal then the "amazing race" was the ultimate spiritual rush. We would be stretching our God-given gifts and talents to the maximum and celebrating life. If the amazing race has no joy, Paul would ask, then where is God?

I press on toward the goal for the prize of the heavenly call of God in Jesus Christ. Let those of us who are mature be of the same mind; and if you think differently about anything, this too God will reveal to you. Only let us hold fast to what we have attained. (Philippians 3: 14-16) and...

Finally, beloved, whatever is true, whatever is honorable, whatever is just, whatever is pure, whatever is pleasing, whatever is commendable, if there is any excellence and if there is anything worthy of praise, think about these things. Keep on doing the things that you have learned and received and heard and seen in me, and the God of peace will be with you. (Philippians 4: 8-9)

A Personal Journey:

I'm happy to admit that I'm a big fan of a very popular television show called "The Amazing Race." It's a show that opens a (fleeting) window on the amazing diversity of our world. But, it's primarily a down-and-dirty primer on how people interact in very stressful, fast-paced competition. Every week we see some example of relationships building or falling apart. We see the best and the worst of teamwork, cooperation, support, and sensitivity as the two-person teams race around the world for a $1 million prize.

A couple of years ago, about midway through the race, a largely dysfunctional team, a dating couple, were eliminated. The man, an athletic thirty-something character, had billed himself as a classic uber-competitor who was virtually destined to win the top prize. In the early weeks of the show, he spent a good portion of his time making key mistakes, acting fierce, and brow-beating his partner, who he didn't feel was "competitive" enough. The woman, it seemed, spent much of her time trying to ensure that her partner didn't spontaneously combust over their various misfortunes.

When they were finally eliminated, the man stared angrily at the ever-present camera and said he wasn't really sure if he could carry forward a relationship with his traveling partner because he needed someone who was just as "competitive" as he was. This woman, apparently, didn't fill the bill.

I don't want to be too hard on Mr. Uber-Competitor. None of us is at our best when we're hot, dirty, hungry, thirsty, and hopelessly lost. Coming in dead last on national television isn't a lot of fun. But, the one lasting legacy, for me anyway, of this ill-fated team is that they made me think about the word "competitive." What does it mean to be competitive? And, particularly, what does it mean to be competitive as a person of faith?

When I was a teenager, my mother would often challenge me to play a unique two-person basketball game called "Twenty-one." Basically, the first person to shoot 21 baskets was the winner. If you scored, you kept the ball. The other person didn't get a chance to score unless you missed a shot. My mother played on a traveling basketball team in her younger days and she was a *very good* basketball player. Once she got going, she seldom missed a shot. This was very annoying for a teenager like me who fancied himself as being good at sports. It wasn't fun to always lose to your mother at "Twenty-one."

But, early on, I realized that my mother's main goal wasn't to beat me. Her main goal was to be the best she could be. She believed in using her God-given gifts to the fullest. And, she was wonderful at encouraging and helping others to use their gifts, whatever they might be.

Why be competitive? What's the purpose of it? Real competitors don't take their joy from pounding their opponents into submission. They take their joy from feeling an exciting harmony of body, mind, and emotions that allows them to perform at the highest level they've been given to perform. I think people of faith "compete" as a thank-you to God. In prayer, we wouldn't thank God for victory over others. We'd thank God for the strength and courage to use the gifts we've been given to their fullest.

It's always been my belief that people who *need* to win in order to briefly quiet their inner demons are not really competitors at all. If we need to pummel others in order to improve our self-image then we have problems that need to be resolved at another level. The best competitors I've ever met felt immeasurable joy when they played at their highest level. And they always had a few tips, sage advice, or a word of encouragement for others. They wanted others to have that same feeling of joy. They wanted others to share what's sometimes called "The Dominating Dream"—setting courageous goals and believing you have the gifts and ability to achieve them.

What does it mean to be competitive as a person of faith? I don't believe it has anything to do with creating some arcane, unfortunate world of winners and losers. I believe it's all about using God's gifts to the fullest—discovering the spiritual joy in what we've received—and carefully, caringly helping others to do the same.

A Time for Reflection:

Reflect on your past experiences with competition. Have there been times when you've felt angry, upset, or humiliated by defeat? Why did you feel those emotions? Are there times when victory caused you to be "full of yourself?" Why?

As a Christian—holding God at the centre of all life—what does competition mean for you? Would you still want to win?

If you had a teammate whose skill level was poor (and he/she is probably hurting your team's ability to compete) what would you do? How would you relate to that person?

Have you ever had "The Dominating Dream" in your life? Describe what this dream is, or could be, for you.

Where do you find genuine joy in the "amazing race" of life? What changes do you need to make in order to transform hassle and anxiety into joy?

If you were to thank God, right now, for your life, what would you say? Why are you thankful?

A Time for Prayer:

Loving God, thank you for the gifts and skills you've given us from your bounty. We thank you for the uniqueness and wonder of the amazing race you've set before us and we dedicate our life travels to you. Forgive us when we try to place ourselves instead of you at the centre of life. Forgive us for the pain it causes to others and to ourselves. Guide us to experience the joy of competition—the wonder of extending our God-given gifts to the furthest degree— and the faith and love to help others experience "success" in the amazing race. Amen.

A Time for Action:

Competition is all around us, in work and at play. Define clearly for yourself what your Christian faith means to you as a competitor and decide in each instance of competition what that faith calls you to be and to do.

Week 18: They Eat Their Leaders, Don't They?

The dustbins of history are filled with the ashes of leaders who have tried and failed. Sometimes they failed because they simply didn't have the instincts or the "royal jelly" to lead. They weren't clear enough or sharp enough or bright enough to see opportunities and make things happen. People couldn't muster any real faith or trust in them. Sometimes circumstances made it impossible for anyone to lead effectively and they just happened to be the unfortunate people on the hot seat. They may have been wonderful, inspirational leaders but the stars were arrayed against them.

Whether successful or unsuccessful, one thing is certain in the life of a leader. Whatever they do, a portion of their community will almost always consider them an ass. Moses is a case in point. Here's a man who, at the call of God, undertook the supremely difficult task of leading an entire people out of Egypt and into the so-called "Promised Land." A noble task. And yet, was there ever a biblical figure who took more flack than Moses? Everything bad that happened was placed on his head. People muttered behind his back and always seemed on the edge of high revolt. How could this man succeed?

But, Moses did succeed. What does that mean for leadership? What made Moses a good leader? It clearly wasn't because he was a hale and popular fellow. We know that he wasn't much of a communicator. But, maybe he just happened to have the right mission at the right time, and the genuine faith and courage to follow through with it. Perhaps the lesson of Moses is that leadership is more about mission than manipulation; more about vision than popularity. You may not want to assume the mantle of leadership, and take all the flack that goes with it, unless you have a God-centred fire to get things done.

As Pharaoh drew near, the Israelites looked back, and there were the Egyptians advancing on them. In great fear the Israelites called out to the Lord. They said to Moses, "Was it because there were no graves in Egypt that you have taken us away to die in the wilderness? What have you done to us, bringing us out of Egypt? Is this not the very thing we told you in Egypt, 'Let us alone and let us serve the Egyptians'? For it would have been better for us to serve the Egyptians than to die in the wilderness."
(Exodus 14: 10-12)

A Personal Journey:

A few years ago, I had an eye-opening conversation with the mayor of a small community north of Toronto. He told me that throughout his decade-long tenure as mayor he had received an unremitting flow of phone calls, at all hours, from unhappy constituents. The streetlight in front of someone's house had gone out. The water pressure in someone's taps didn't seem as strong as last week. The neighbour's dog was howling in the middle of the night. The complaints ran from the sublime to the ridiculous. But, in each case, the kindly mayor calmly noted the complaint and assured the angry citizen that he'd look into it. And he did.

More recently, I was talking to a religious leader who was shepherding his congregation through some difficult decisions about their future. He said being a leader had many requirements but, without question, it's a tough row to hoe if you don't have a very thick skin. If the congregation's decisions followed one course, half his members would be convinced that "the minister had to go." If decisions went the opposite way, the other half would be after his head. Whatever he said, whatever course he struck, he was destined to be the "villain" in some people's books.

In these cynical days, when community leaders are often accorded the same respect and affection we feel for dinnertime telemarketers, I think the mayor and the minister deliver two simple but critical messages about leadership.

First, while we may think it's unfair and unreasonable for the poor mayor to field calls from hostile constituents at 3:00 o'clock in the morning, that's not really the point. The point, I think, is that this mayor loved his community so much that he was willing to suffer some tough, unfair, and unreasonable things in order to serve it. Remember, he'd been on the job for ten years! Angry phone calls at ungodly hours didn't scare him away. Leaders who don't lead from a fundamental love of their communities are not leaders. They may want to be leaders; they may like the idea of leadership and title. But, without a genuine love for their community, their cause is already lost.

The second message comes from the minister. And, it's not just about having thick skin. I think his message is that you can't lead without having a vision for your community. Leadership isn't about pleasing everyone, putting out emotional "grassfires," and generally keeping the peace. Authentic leadership is about having a broader vision of the future, inspiring others, making plans, and guiding the community into a better place. Leaders have to live with the fact that part of their community will always resist change. Many people aren't willing to risk the upheaval of trying to find a better place and they'll lay their anger on the leader's head.

I don't pretend to be a great expert on leadership. But, I believe the people who do it well do it with a profound love for their community, an unshakable vision for the future—and, oh yes, a very thick skin.

And one final point. When we see examples of corruption and malfeasance in government (remember the Sponsorship Scandal?) it's easy to tar all our leaders with the same brush. Politicians are always way down the list when polls are taken about who Canadians find most trustworthy in our society. But, such tarring is unfair. Certainly, we need to have a keen eye for shady, self-serving practices locally, regionally, and nationally in Canada. But, we also need to celebrate the vast majority of our leaders who do, in fact, love their community and who do, in fact, have a vision for its future. If we can't show our respect for leaders who've earned it, how can we expect to attract honourable, respectable leaders in the future? If we can't celebrate public service, how will we engage our best and brightest to lead us in the years and decades ahead?

A Time for Reflection:

Think of a leader (he or she doesn't have to be famous) who you've felt great respect for. What qualities did this leader have which stood out for you?

Why do you think people offer themselves up as leaders? What reasons do they give? What reasons might be less obvious?

In churches and other organizations would you rather "fill the role" or leave it vacant until the right leader comes along? What are the advantages and disadvantages of both decisions?

What's the difference between caretaker leadership and visionary leadership? What are the advantages and disadvantages of each? Who would you rather follow and why?

If you were out in the wilderness with Moses, with all the hardships and worries, what would you be saying to your neighbour right now?

Do you think our society's attitudes toward political leaders are fair? How do you personally feel about these leaders? If your son or daughter wanted to enter politics what would you say to him or her?

Under what circumstances would you become a leader in your organization or your community? What would you bring to the leadership role?

A Time for Prayer:

Loving God, open us to understanding the power of leadership in our lives. If you have given us the fire to lead, we pray for the courage to accept our call and the wisdom to engage our community in a powerful vision and a faithful mission. If we are called to support our leaders, may we do so without cynicism, jealously, or disdain. Help us to genuinely understand the vision and joyfully work for the mission which you have set out for us. Amen.

A Time for Action:

If you have a vision, a mission, and the fire for leadership in your heart then it's time to put away the excuses, discuss the implications with family and friends, and follow your call. Why are you waiting? Will the call be any clearer tomorrow? If, like most of us, you're not called to be a leader, why not strip away the useless cynicism you feel about the "system" and take the risk of working for a politician or other leader who is trying to make a difference?

Week 19: A Capacity to Love

The biblical story of Ruth is a wonderful lesson in what it means for human beings to genuinely love one another.

Naomi, her husband, and their two sons are forced by famine to move from Judah to the neighbouring land of Moab. The two sons marry Moabite women. Then, tragically, Noami's husband and her two sons die, leaving her in a strange land with two daughters-in-law, Orpah and Ruth. By this time, things are improving back in Judah and Naomi decides her only real option is to return home. Orpah and Ruth are fully prepared to leave their homeland and go back to Judah with Naomi.

This is where the story takes a very human, very loving twist. Even though Naomi would benefit from the support of her daughters-in-law, she feels they would both be much better off and better cared for in their home country. In spite of her own wants and needs, she tells them to stay in Moab. Her love outweighs her need. Orpah, who genuinely loves Naomi, decides it's best to return to her own people. But, Ruth's love and devotion to Naomi are so intense that she refuses to leave, no matter what pain and uncertainty the future might bring.

Ruth's commitment, her enormous capacity to love, is an extraordinary model for us today. How many of us can feel the depth of emotion which underlies Ruth's love for Naomi—a love captured in one of Scripture's most moving passages?

So she (Naomi) said, "See, your sister-in-law has gone back to her people and to her gods; return after your sister-in-law." But Ruth said, "Do not press me to leave you or to turn back from following you! Where you go I will go; where you lodge I will lodge; your people shall be my people, and your God my God. Where you die, I will die— there will I be buried. May the Lord do thus and so to me, and more as well, if even death parts me from you!" When Naomi saw that she was determined to go with her, she said no more to her. (Ruth 1: 15-18)

A Personal Journey:

In the run-up to Mother's Day, I want to write a few words about mothers (and fathers) and the stereotypes we sometimes hold about them. I want to write a few words about "successful parenting" with the understanding that I'm no expert on the subject and you'd be wise to take this Salter with a grain of salt.

When I was growing up (this would be shortly after the invention of the wheel), there was a very distinct idea of what a mother should be like. Most of the television shows we watched at the time portrayed mothers as stay-at-home people with no profession and few job skills, hobbies, or interests. A mother's work was to keep the house in good order, clean, scrub, and care for her children. And, oh yes, at the end of the day they were supposed to look beautiful and attend to the needs of their poor, tired husbands when they returned from a hard day of pushing paper at the office. The mother's life, according to our television, started and stopped with the care and feeding of her husband and children.

There were countless magazines and books published that defined the proper etiquette for the subservient wife and mother to follow in what was supposed to be "a man's world."

The thing I remember most clearly from my own childhood is that my mother was nothing like the docile TV moms. She obviously didn't read the right magazines or watch the right television shows, because she actually seemed to lead a different life. While she loved her family dearly, she was also a public school teacher, a leader in church and community, and a ferocious basketball player who was unbeatable in a game of "Twenty-one" (see Week 17). She didn't take a back seat to anyone and that was just fine in our family.

The point here is that my own mother didn't fit the mould of her day. And she was certainly not alone in breaking the stereotype. There were many different ways to live out the role of "mother" even in that ultra-conservative era. That's something to celebrate, both then and now. Today, we can celebrate the fact we aren't locked into any stereotypes of what a mother (or father) has to be. There's no hidebound book of etiquette. There is no one way to be a good parent.

Mothers and fathers work outside the home and/or they work in the home. They pursue hobbies or careers or they do volunteer work. Successful families take many shapes—sometimes a single parent, sometimes two, sometimes a large extended family, and sometimes little or no extended family at all. There are as many twists and turns as there are families.

We also celebrate the part of our society today that holds up parenting as a key value. We celebrate the families where men have finally buried the notion that it's "a man's world" and are becoming full partners in the work of family.

What do we celebrate most of all about successful parenting today? We can certainly celebrate the breaking of stereotypes, wherever we see it happening. But, more than that, successful parenting is a celebration of our capacity to love. It's the greatest of human gifts for a son or daughter to look back and say, "Mom (Dad), you did it your way. You did it the best way you knew how. You gave us your heart and sometimes we broke it. You gave it to us again. You gave us opportunities and sometimes we threw them back at you. You offered them again. We thank you for being yourself and for loving us in spite of it all—because of it all.

A Time for Reflection:

Discuss Naomi, Orpah, and Ruth in terms of their "capacity to love." What qualities do you see in each of them that you believe are part of a loving person's character?

Discuss the parenting and gender stereotypes you grew up with. What impact did they have on the way you think and act as an adult today?

Do you feel that we still hold onto parenting and gender stereotypes today? Where do you see changes happening? Are male and female parenting roles changing?

Discuss your own capacity to love. How does that "capacity" play out in your day to day parenting responsibilities? Does "love" sometimes seem like an uphill battle? How do you cope when the going gets tough?

At the end of the day, if someone was to speak admiringly of you and say, 'He (she) is a successful parent because....' how would you like them to finish that sentence?

A Time for Prayer:

Loving God, hold us in your hands and shape us into people who have the genuine capacity to love.

Where we've offered our hearts and had them broken, give us the courage to offer them again. Where we've offered opportunity and hope and had them thrown back in our faces, grant us the faith to offer them again. Gracious God, loving Parent, grant us the compassion to bring your love with us into the darkest, most difficult, most painful places of our lives. Grant us the wisdom for great hope and the capacity for great love. Amen.

A Time for Action:

Parenting is one of the most important things we can do in life. It's also a very sensitive subject that is seldom shared and discussed with others beyond the immediate family. It's easy to become isolated as a parent. To avoid isolation, and to honour the importance of the subject, start or join a parenting group in order to share and learn from others and to connect with the best literature available on the subject.

Week 20: There's Something Sacred in Your Garden

Jesus grew up in a largely rural, agrarian society. Much of what he said, the verbal images he used, reflected the fact he was talking to people who knew full well what it meant to plant crops, tend orchards, and raise livestock. In making his points about the Kingdom of God, Jesus connected with his followers by talking about a lost sheep, or wheat and chaff, or sowing seeds, or a tree and its fruit. Jesus' parables and sayings were strongly centred in the real world where people lived. If you could dig in the dirt, if you could raise a crop, if you could husband livestock, if you could keep an orchard healthy, then Jesus' words might well strike a cord with you. Most of us today aren't farmers or ranchers, but many of us still have some kind of primordial need to dig in the dirt and see things grow. We're gardeners. And we intrinsically understand there's something vital, something sacred about the earth. Jesus still speaks to us through the natural world. The dirt in our fingernails still offers messages about God's Kingdom today.

Beware of false prophets, who come to you in sheep's clothing but inwardly are ravenous wolves. You will know them by their fruits. Are grapes gathered from thorns, or figs from thistles? In the same way, every good tree bears good fruit, but the bad tree bears bad fruit. A good tree cannot bear bad fruit, nor can a bad tree bear good fruit. Every tree that does not bear good fruit is cut down and thrown into the fire. Thus you will know them by their fruits.   (Matthew 7: 15-20)

A Personal Journey:

After visiting a number of greenhouses and slogging around in our backyard flower beds last weekend, my wife and I got into a discussion about why we enjoy gardening so much. After all, it's not the cheapest pastime in the world, it can be hard on the back, and at any given time you can be knee-deep in dirt, manure, peat moss, or mulch.

So why do we enjoy it? We decided we like to garden because it's something that focuses all of our attention. When we garden, the giant list of "things to accomplish this weekend" is set aside. The burgeoning busyness of daily life is much less important than the opportunity to dig in the dirt and plant things. Gardening is our chance to let go of the things that tie us up in knots. It represents something primal in life, something sacred. In a world where our footprints are often broad and clumsy, gardening is a chance to touch the earth with our hands and feel surrounded and refreshed by God's spirit.

It would be sad if gardening was seen only as a temporary escape from the general frustrations of day-to-day living; a temporary respite before we're sent back into "the real game of life." In fact, my wife and I decided that just the opposite is true. Far from being a temporary fix, gardening is a powerful metaphor to help us understand what "the real game of life" can be and should be. It's not an escape from life at all. It's a metaphor that can help us explore healthy living in a sometimes unhealthy world. There is something sacred in the garden.

I wish I could offer up all the metaphorical messages of the garden. I'm sure they're boundless. But, it seems to me the messages revolve around what it means to walk in the world with a high degree of care and patience—probably more than we're accustomed to feeling.

For example, let's take the proverbial "good idea." How many times have we seen someone in a small group or committee throw off a wonderful new idea and then sit back contentedly, waiting for it to take life. As often as not, it goes nowhere and the proponent is frustrated and upset. I'll never waste another good idea on this group, they might think.

But, if we're gardening, we'd never throw seeds or plants onto uncultivated ground. What would we expect to happen?

Gardeners prepare the ground for their good ideas. They talk to people in advance. They send e-mails; they have their good idea written out and discussed long before decisions need to be made. The ground is made fertile. If the "good idea" is capable of taking root, it will.

Gardeners—all those who see something sacred in the garden—have the opportunity to live the metaphor of care and patience in all their relationships. Similar to a "good idea," a relationship can't grow if no thought is given to how and where and why it's planted. A relationship can't survive if no one is willing to protect it from a freezing cold night or a burning hot day. A relationship can't survive without being fed and watered. No relationship can be faulted for growing slowly and none should be despised for not growing at all.

Importantly, the gardener knows that there is a cycle of life. What grows and bears fruit will lie down at the end of its season. And still the garden must be prepared, made ready for the cycle of life to begin again.

The garden is sacred because it's wrapped in God's spirit. Everywhere there are messages about life and living, about caring and patience. The metaphor of the garden isn't about escaping life. It's about discovering life and living it abundantly.

A Time for Reflection:

What are your memories of the garden (or the farm or the ranch) when you were a child? What life lessons did the natural world teach you? Was there some place, or some time, where you uniquely felt the presence of God?

What does your garden mean to you today? Describe how it makes you feel. Do you consider it "sacred?"

Describe exactly what steps you would follow to make your garden grow.

Describe exactly what steps you would follow to help a relationship grow.

Describe exactly what steps you would follow to help make your best idea sink strong roots and flourish.

"The gardener knows that there is a cycle of life." What does the "cycle of life" mean and how does it influence the way you live your life?

A Time for Prayer:

Loving God, help us find you in the garden. As we rub the soil between our fingers help us celebrate the miracle of life and growth. Help us find Christ in the sun and the rain and the green shoots that grow bigger each day. In your sacred garden, God, teach us about caring and patience. Teach us how to be good gardeners throughout your entire world—lovers of abundance and joyful students of life in your kingdom. We praise you and honour you, gracious God. We sing your thanksgiving every day. Amen.

A Time for Action:

Even if you've never done it before, plant a garden and care for it. Let God talk to you in the garden. Every step of the way, make your garden a metaphor for how God really wants you to live your life.

Week 21: Technology is a Gift, Not a God

Technology is a constantly changing and always amazing aspect of our modern lives. Things we couldn't even imagine a few years ago are now commonplace. Everything from intricate laser surgery to MP3 players to multi-faceted communication tools that fit in the palm of your hand are available—and on the cusp of becoming outdated almost as soon as they appear on the scene. Technology is a fast-paced, highly competitive business where all things are possible; where the only limit is the human imagination.

This landslide of technological innovation is both wonderful and worrisome for human society. Have our ethical understandings kept pace with the technological explosion around us? Do we have the wisdom to determine when not to do something even though we have the technological ability to accomplish it? Should we create human life? Should we sustain life because we *can*—even when there is no quality of life? Should we use technology for military superiority or for peace? Should we use computer technology to dominate or communicate? What happens to a world of exploding technological innovation if it's not coupled with the power of wisdom?

Happy are those who find wisdom, and those who get understanding, for her income is better than silver, and her revenue better than gold. She is more precious than jewels, and nothing you desire can compare with her. Long life is in her right hand; in her left hand are riches and honor. Her ways are ways of pleasantness, and all her paths are peace. She is a tree of life to those who lay hold of her; those who hold her fast are called happy. (Proverbs 3: 13-18)

A Personal Journey:

I'm not very good with automated banking machines. I admit that. For many years, I avoided them in the resolute belief that they would never catch on. Today, while I still prefer banking with human beings, I *have* learned how to draw cash from one ancient bank machine—when I need to—after hours.

Last week, giddy with my repeated successes at cash withdrawal, I ventured into the uncharted territory of transferring money between accounts. The ancient bank machine, which I had come to trust, made ominous noises and offered up such a range of account numbers and options that I was seized with panic and could only stare hopelessly at the screen.

"Do you need more time?" the machine asked me. Beneath the courteous question I could sense impatience. I pushed the "yes" button, if only to delay the inevitable. Twenty seconds later the machine asked again, "Do you need more time?"

Defeated, I stared at the screen until it defaulted back to the beginning.

"What would you like to do?" it challenged. There was no button that said "run for help" or just "run" so I continued to stare. Eventually, frustrated and disgusted, the ancient bank machine coughed up my bank card and the ordeal was over. I shuffled away into the dark night, humbled and humiliated.

Not everyone is as hopeless at automated banking as I am. Most people make their transactions smoothly and efficiently and their automated banking machines have little reason to cajole or criticize them.

I admit my failings. It's just that sometimes, when I come face to face with an automated banking machine, it makes me wonder who's the boss? Who is, after all, in charge of this machine and all the technology that grows and expands and constantly changes the way we live and do business?

Specifically, I wonder at the reverence our society seems to hold for technology as the great hope for the future. Technology is often celebrated for making the workplace more efficient. The "good news" seems to be that one high-tech machine has eliminated 50 jobs and the company is now much more profitable. For whom is this "good news?" Certainly not for the 50 people who have lost their jobs. By extension, it seems the best possible news would be that high-tech machines have eliminated all jobs everywhere, profits are through the roof, and the only human task left is for the owner to push the "on" button.

Personally, I believe that *people* are the great hope for the future. If a technological advance eliminates five jobs, I can understand and accept that. Society moves on. Jobs do become obsolete. But, if a technological advance eliminates five jobs I'd like to be sure that it creates six. That tells me who's in control.

From a faith perspective, it's hard not to see technology as one of God's great gifts. It has the potential to enhance our human existence in countless ways. But, it's just a tool. It has no intrinsic value and no intrinsic power. Its value and power depend on how we use it. I think we can get into some very big trouble when we try to make technology into a god rather than a gift. If we let technology take control, if we consider it the ultimate value, we run the risk of losing ourselves.

If I ever visit my ancient bank machine again, I'm going to stand up proudly and take all the time I need! You may not like it, my technological "friend," but you work for me!

A Time for Reflection:

Describe how the technological explosion that surrounds us every day makes you feel in your day to day life. Does it excite you? Worry you? Confuse you? Why?

What does the word "wisdom" mean to you as a person of faith?

Do you think our society has the wisdom not to do something even though we may have the technological ability to make it happen? What, in your mind, is "good" technology? Examples? What is "bad" technology? Examples? How do you go about deciding which is which?

Do you think humanity should develop and implement the medical technology to create human life? Why or why not?

What do you think about technology that puts people out of work? Under what circumstances is it a good thing...a bad thing?

It was stated above that technology is one of God's great gifts to humanity. If you believe this to be true what does it mean for the way you live and interact with others on a day to day basis?

A Time for Prayer:

Gracious God, giver of every good and loving gift, help us to understand the gift of technology. Guide us to understand its place in your world and to use it as a tool for peace, justice, and reconciliation. Loving

God, help us to apply the wonders of technology to the kingdom responsibilities of eliminating poverty, renewing the environment, and fighting economic, social, and political oppression. Forgive us when we make technology into a god and surrender our moral and ethical powers to treat it as a gift and use it well. Help us to remember, God, that if its use doesn't honour you then technology is hurting our brothers and sisters and stripping all our lives of value. Amen.

A Time for Action:

Define for yourself what constitutes "bad technology" (the negative, destructive use of technology) in God's world. Its impact might be medical/scientific, military, sociological, environmental, etc. etc. Choose a specific "impact" that you feel passionate about. Write letters to the editor of your local newspaper. Contact your Member of Parliament and the government minister connected to your concern. Start or join a group of like-minded people who are keeping the issue in the public eye. You can make a difference if you focus yourself on one key issue and work hard.

Week 22: It's So Hard to Let Go

I formally retired as a United Church minister in 2007 after nearly 27 years on the job. During that time, I "officiated" at countless funerals, piling up a mountain of words intended to comfort people who, by and large, were in no mood to be comforted. I had the words and I had the scripture passages designed to get us through the awkward, painful rite of passage known as the funeral service. But, I was essentially disengaged. I was the necessary functionary for a necessary event. I was sympathetic, but not really involved. I hoped that the plethora of words and scripture passages meant something to the bereaved, because to me they seemed rote and empty.

They seemed rote and empty until my mother died, and, a few years later, my father. It was then that I listened. It was then that I let the soothing melody of the Psalms wash over me and give me comfort. It was then that I felt God's presence in the search for meaning and closure, in the need to let go—if not now, then sometime down the road. God was present in the words, not just during the services, but in the words of friends and family before and after. God was there in people's desire to be present, even if they said nothing. When they looked at me they showed the face of God. It took the death of my parents to teach me how to measure love by presence and listen to the true rhythm of the Psalms for the first time.

I lift up my eyes to the hills—from where will my help come? My help comes from the Lord, who made heaven and earth. He will not let your foot be moved; he who keeps you will not slumber. He who keeps Israel will neither slumber nor sleep. The Lord is your keeper; the Lord is your shade at your right hand. The sun shall not strike you by day, nor the moon by night. The Lord will keep you from all evil; he will keep your life. The Lord will keep your going out and your coming in from this time on and forevermore. (Psalm 121)

A Personal Journey:

My father is very sick. At 90 years of age his vital organs are slowly shutting down on him and he'll die soon. Doctors are much better at preserving life than predicting death so we don't know if it'll be next week, or the week after, or the week after that. We just know that he'll die soon.

Death isn't a particularly new concept. But it always seems unfamiliar. It shadows life, lying in the bushes, and rising up to frighten us even though we knew it was there all along.

I suppose when death rises up and stares us in the face, we all deal with it differently.

As a stoic male, like my father, I deal with it badly. All my emotions are bunched and jangled and poorly exercised. It's as if they've all been stuffed into a small balloon, slipping out in dribs and drabs without coherent pattern or expression. As awkward, foolish, and painful as it might seem, I will not let the balloon break.

It seems too surreal, the advent of death. Is there some combination of words and feelings that can adequately account for all those years of relationship? Perhaps there's something in the silences, or in our last halting conversation, that holds the truth. But, it seems the truth would have been told long ago.

For the last two weeks I've avoided all thoughts of death by focusing on the medicine; the amazing technologies of treatment. There are antibiotics for infection, tubes for drainage, oxygen for breathing, and morphine for comfort. Machines inexorably measure Dad's slow decline. Does he have enough of this; or too much of that? Is there something else to try?

Once in awhile, memory creeps in. There are the good moments when my father isn't a dying ember but a big, strong man of visions, dreams, and vitality.

I picture him creating a basketball court 45 years ago—building a backboard from scratch, attaching it to a pole, and raising it all into place with brute strength as the sweat rolls off his body. I picture him playing catch with me in the backyard or meticulously tying fishing flies in the basement.

I see him on the porch during a thunderstorm, telling me about his life and his hero, Jack London. I picture his volcanic temper rising to explosion and then disappearing without a trace.

I remember his athleticism—his love for baseball—and his sense of humour. "I was a one o'clock hitter," he used to say about his prowess in batting practice. "Unfortunately, the games didn't start until two."

Why are these isolated memories breaking in?

I'm beginning to think that they come with a message attached—and a command to listen more carefully. I think they're saying that the time is fast approaching when I need to let go.

I don't think my own emotional bubble is going to burst any time soon, but I need to let Dad go—let him fall into the arms of his own destiny. I'll still fight for him. I'll fight to retrieve all the memories that I've too easily let slip away. Even though his body has withered and will soon die, we'll still laugh together for years to come.

With the help of memory, I understand that it will soon be time to let Dad go. But, I'm jealous for his spirit. I want it to stay close by. I want it to surround my children and my children's children with the joy of life.

Is that too much to ask of God?

A Time for Reflection:

Write down five words that "death" brings into your mind. Why have you chosen these five and why do they have meaning for you?

If you've lost a loved one, what did people do that brought you comfort? What did you do for yourself that brought comfort; that helped you to let go?

What is "closure" for you in the loss of a loved one? How do you reach it? Why is "closure" such a different concept than "comfort?"

What part do memories have in the healing process? Are memories always healing?

What is your concept of spirit? What does it mean to say "I want his/her spirit to stay close by?" Is that real or possible?

Where do you see God in the loss of a loved one? Where is God in the process of comfort, healing, and closure?

A Time for Prayer:

Loving God, open us to the truths of family and friends who have returned into your loving heart. May we continue to hear what was good and just in their spirits and forgive what was not. May we fight for their memories and carry them from generation to generation so that their time on earth can be marked and their spirits heard. In Christ's name we pray. Amen.

A Time for Action:

Imagine that you are sitting in a room with a loved one who has passed away. Amazingly, they are "alive" for you in just this one moment. What questions would you have? Ask them. What wisdom would they have for your life today? When you leave the room, what spirit do you feel you want to take away with you?

Week 23: Some Species Eat Their Young

When you ask a professional counselor what he or she believes to be the first rule of counseling, the answer may surprise you. You may expect the counselor to talk about seating arrangements, words and phrases to avoid, progress reports, or measuring success. But, a counselor will tell you that the first rule of counseling is, above all, to do no harm.

When you reflect on it, "doing no harm" is a pretty strong starting point for all of our relationships. What if the first rule of child-raising was "Above all, do no harm?" It would mean taking a serious look at how we relate to our children on a day to day basis. Berating, brow-beating, belittling, and criticizing them "for their own good" would be automatically forbidden. Living vicariously through our children would be off limits. Ignoring or avoiding them also breaks the rule. "Doing no harm" sounds pretty simple in the context of all the psychological and sociological bafflespeak floating around these days. But, that's a good thing. It's basic and fundamental. It's at the heart of human relationships. If we're doing something that causes harm, then we need to stop it. Somewhere at the heart of love itself is a fundamental spirit that says "Above all, do no harm."

Owe no one anything, except to love one another; for the one who loves another has fulfilled the law. The commandments, "You shall not commit adultery; You shall not murder; You shall not steal;

You shall not covet"; and any other commandment, are summed up in this word, "Love your neighbor as yourself." Love does no wrong to a neighbor; therefore, love is the fulfilling of the law. (Romans 13: 8-10)

A Personal Journey:

Some species, apparently, feel they have no choice but to eat their young. These species aren't good role models. Their parenting skills seem weak and, clearly, this isn't the best way to deal with teenage rebellion.

Human beings do not eat their young. We've decided that the best way to deal with our young, particularly our teenagers, is to complain about them. We don't eat our young, we just nibble. Adult humans are always "going on" about how teenagers are careless, lazy, disrespectful, slothful, and totally lacking in ambition. Worse than that, these terrible teens refuse to sit and listen to the wisdom of their elders.

The amazing thing about adults is that we're totally oblivious to those heady days when we were teenagers ourselves. We've blotted out the misanthropic adults of our teenage years who complained that we were careless, lazy, disrespectful, slothful, and totally lacking in ambition. Those adults, whoever they were, totally misunderstood us.

There's a very real possibility that the age-old practice of nibbling at young people is one of those age-old practices that never did make any sense. A recent poll of teenage attitudes shows, as these polls do time and again, that teenagers value hard work, dedication, and commitment as much as adults value them.

Teenagers have goals, dreams, and ambitions. And, according to all the polls, the people they most respect are their parents. My guess is that the poll results wouldn't have been much different for my generation of teens or yours.

Teenagers are working hard to find their way in a very complex world. Some are struggling. Some are lashing out. The vast majority is prospering and our society is always benefiting from their enthusiasm and their compassion.

Being human, we adults are always going to nibble, just a little bit. But, we also need to take a reality pill and start valuing all of our young people. Whether they're prospering or whether they're struggling and lashing out, they're a critically important part of our community, not just for the future, but right now.

Putting teenagers down has never been an option. It has never been fair. But, in a world as fast-paced, challenging, and dangerous as it is for teens today, they need a community behind them; a community that supports them and cheers their every success.

A Time for Reflection:

Discuss the whole philosophy behind the phrase "Above all, do no harm." Is it enough to live by? Do you agree that this phrase can be found at the heart of genuine human love? Why?

How were you raised? Was the spirit of "do no harm" part of your family home?

How do the child-raising "models" you experienced as a child influence the models you use with your own children?

Does the poll on teenage attitudes mentioned above surprise you? How does it agree or disagree with your own feelings about teenagers? How did society treat you when you were a teenager? How did you feel about that treatment?

What do you think this week's scripture means when it says, "Owe no one anything, except to love one another?"

What do you think it means for a community to build respect for teenagers not only as "our future" but as a key part of our present life together.

A Time for Prayer:

Loving God, teach us what it means in your gracious kingdom to do no harm. Help us to place those words and that spirit into the heart of a self-giving love that heals and brings wholeness to ourselves and to others. Gracious God, we understand how critical it is to love our neighbour with the same degree of concern we have for our own well-being. Guide us, we pray, to walk in the world as parents, friends, partners, and citizens who can see the face of God in all of humanity. Amen.

A Time for Action:

Find ways to support the youth in your community. You can support a local teen centre or church youth group with your money and/or with your volunteer time. Ensure the voices of young people are heard where decisions are being made. If there is conflict, respect the fact all sides should be heard. Encourage and support youth initiatives in the community. Remember that your "neighbour," in the context of your faith, can also be your own child.

Week 24: Naked Ladies and Other Laughing Matters

When did our churches become the places where fun goes to die? When did we decide that laughter and spontaneity were a smudge on the Body of Christ? Why does a soaring hymn like "Joyful, Joyful We Adore You" sound like a funeral dirge when we sing it?

These questions may sound a little flip, even a little unfair, to some churches. But, they're worth thinking about. At their core, they're tough questions that serve to challenge what we actually believe. If we believe in God's love and the strength and freedom it gives us to use our gifts and talents in the world, why do we appear so morose in worship? Do we believe that Christ is joy or not? Is worship a celebration of God's gifts to us or is it a chore to be endured; a gold star on our "to do" list?

What would happen if we set aside one complete Sunday for laughter? Our only purpose would be to make one another laugh and we'd dedicate it all to God as a thank-offering for all we've been given. Would anybody come? Would anybody be able to find God in the laughter?

For everything there is a season, and a time for every matter under heaven: a time to be born, and a time to die; a time to plant, and a time to pluck up what is planted; a time to kill, and a time to heal; a time to break down and a time to build up; a time to weep, and a time to laugh; a time to mourn, and a time to dance... (Ecclesiastes 3: 1-4)

A Personal Journey:

I hesitate to tell this sexually-charged story to such solid, upstanding readers as yourselves, but the time has come to tell the sordid truth.

When I was 12 years old, I happened to wander into the living room of our house just in time to see my mother and a group of her women friends huddled around a large, green book. This was obviously not your average book. The women were 'ooooing' and 'ahhhhing' over one particular page as if it was a gilded invitation to tea at the royal palace.

Suddenly, Mrs. Albright, our next door neighbour, shouted out, "Isn't that the most gorgeous naked lady you've ever seen!" At that point, the little conclave of middle-aged women had my undivided attention. A *naked lady*, I thought—right here in my house! I don't care if it's just a picture. This is very good!

So, I positioned myself back in the hallway, out of sight. Eventually, my mother placed the big green book on our bookshelf and I memorized the spot.

The only thing left was to gather the troops. I went through the neighbourhood bragging that I knew where to find a picture of a naked lady that would knock their socks off. As you can imagine, it wasn't hard to gather a crowd of excited 12-year-old boys to my back door. Surreptitiously, we inched through the kitchen and into the living room. I pulled the big green book off the shelf and the boys surrounded me. The floral design on the cover surprised me a bit, but I moved on. Inside, there we many pictures of flowers: asters, geraniums, zinnias, and more. Where could this naked lady be? Finally, I saw it. The "Naked Lady" was a colourful, shapely flower that fairly lept off the page. Unfortunately, it didn't seem to bear much resemblance to its namesake. The boys snorted with contempt and quietly left the house.

Humiliated, I sat on the couch and hung my head. I'll never live this one down, I thought. I'm going to have to find a whole new set of friends. Within a few minutes my mother came into the room and sat next to me, and since my life was over anyway, I unleashed the whole sordid tale. She had the oddest reaction. She laughed. She laughed and she laughed some more. At first, it made me mad. Then, after a few moments, the laughter started to tickle me. I started to laugh, too. I laughed at myself and it felt good. Suddenly, the whole incident felt like what it was—a funny little thing that happens to you on the way to growing up.

I mention this little event because it's the first time I ever recognized the healing power of laughter. I believe laughter is one of the greatest gifts God has ever given us for the healing of body, mind, and spirit. The ability to laugh at ourselves, at our own faults and foibles, signals a critical openness to healing.

This laughter offers us three things. First, it's a sign of self-recognition. It says, 'Yes, I'm fallible and I can do foolish and silly things. I am absolutely and completely imperfect and I know it! Second, it's a sign of self-acceptance and forgiveness. It says, 'In spite of my faults there's a deep joy inside over who I am. I'm not ready to let that joy be overcome.' Finally, laughter says, 'I have the power to change, to find healthier ways to be who God has given me to be.'

God gives us the unique ability to laugh at ourselves. It's a profoundly healing gift. It has the wonderful potential to help us love who we are and celebrate what we can be. I discovered this gift many years ago while searching for a beautiful naked lady and it continues to amaze me each day of my life.

A Time for Reflection:

Why do many (if not most) churches have such a hard time expressing joy and laughter in worship?

What's holding them back from feeling joy in the Lord?

How does it feel in your church? Is worship dark and sad or is it celebratory? How would you like it to be and why? What encourages you and what holds you back in finding joyful worship?

Have you ever had a "naked lady" event that helped you gain fresh perspective on life? Can you share it?

Discuss laughter as a healing gift from God. When is it healing? When is it not healing? Can laughter change lives?

Let's assume that being able to both *love who you are* and *celebrate who you can be* is a good thing. Is it hard to get to that place in your life? What stands in the way? Where is God in the process?

A Time for Prayer:

Loving, laughing God, strip away the fear from our lives and open us to the power of joy. Where there is negativity, help us stand up for hope. Where there is cynicism, help us be Christ for others. Where there is surrender, help us stand beside our brothers and sisters, waiting to see your face and feel your guiding hand. Gracious God, may we live with healing laughter, letting it purify us of arrogance and pride, so that we can work for the Kingdom and walk with joy in the world. Amen.

A Time for Action:

Arrange for a play, skit, monologue, or dialogue that brings laughter to your worship service while also bringing a faithful message. Encourage your worship committee, with the help of other creative people in your congregation, to find more and more ways (plays, special music, bands, singing groups, audio-visuals, presentations, etc. etc.) to make worship more joyful and celebratory. Give people opportunities to talk about what joyful worship means to them so that the issue is front and centre with your congregation. If you dare, organize a "Laughter Sunday" as a thank-offering to God.

Week 25: The Incredible Lightness of Letting Go

As a species, we humans aren't very good at letting things go. I receive confirmation of this statement every time I take a look at our basement storage area. "Things" are piled upon "things" and only a tiny fraction of them have any use whatsoever in the modern world. Some "things" never got unpacked from our arrival here in 1989. The truth is, useless as they are, we *own* these things; we *control* these things. To throw them out would be to stop owning them, to surrender control. That's hard to do when control is such a compelling social value in our world.

In fact, "letting go" is one thing at which very few of us are accomplished. We are a people who keep mental lists of real or imagined slights and hold grudges. We have passionate dislikes and forgive only with great difficulty. Letting go requires a surrender of control. If we let them go, we no longer own and control the grudges, dislikes, and biases that serve to define us. How do we let go? And what comes back into the space we've created?

Who will separate us from the love of Christ? Will hardship, or distress, or persecution, or famine, or nakedness, or peril, or sword? No, in all these things we are more than conquerors through him who loved us. For I am convinced that neither death, nor life, nor angels, nor rulers, nor things present, nor things to come, nor powers, nor height, nor depth, nor anything else in all creation,

*will be able to separate us from the love of God in
Christ Jesus our Lord.* (Romans 8: 35, 37-39)

A Personal Journey:

Over the last few months I've been thinking about
the word "control." It never dawned on me before how
much power that word has had in my life—perhaps all
our lives. From my earliest years, there was always
someone (parent, teacher, friend, or neighbour)
demanding that I "get a grip," "toe the line," or "please
control myself." I was being groomed for polite
society. We're all taught how to more graciously
manipulate the levers of self-control and other-control
in order to get what we want. It seems to be part of
our socialization process, with a well-developed
system of rewards along the way.

Of course, as we get older, the demand for control
gets more sophisticated. We "manage" our
environment. We learn the best techniques for getting
others to behave as we want them to. We manipulate
our lives and our world to get the things we decide we
need. The "winners" are the ones who control the
most "things." The losers? The "losers" are often
trying to figure out what it takes to be a "winner." It's
all about being on the right side of more and more
sophisticated systems of self-control and other-
control.

Into this little paradigm of control trots the little
Trojan horse of faith. For the longest time I saw the
church and religion as just another mechanism of
control; a set of rules to follow which eventually led to
a fine reward. The rules were "good" or, at least,
benign, and they constituted a more kindly
methodology for self-control and other-control than I
could find in the general population. So I thought, if
you're going to choose a control system, the church is
as good as any, and better than most.

It shows you how wrong you can be. The little Trojan horse comes with a big surprise. With some help from my friends, I've come to realize that genuine faith has virtually nothing to do with manipulation and control. Just the opposite, really. It has to do with "letting go"; releasing all those things we "need" to control into the heart of a higher power. It has to do with trusting that this higher power will replace our incessant battle for control with a new spirit that's healing and life-giving. Faith is about a radical new paradigm for life. Instead of doing everything in our power to gain control, faith is about giving it up; letting it go, surrendering it to God. It's believing that God will fill the void with much better things.

Is "letting go" just plain laziness? Is it an excuse for doing nothing? The Apostle Paul was a great believer in "letting go and letting God." He was energized to travel the Roman world, enduring constant hardships, to spread the good news about Jesus Christ. "Letting go" isn't an excuse for inactivity. It's a way of saying our life is focused on creating, not controlling. "Letting go" is one of the hardest, most challenging pieces of work we can ever take on. If you doubt this, just try to let go of a heartfelt resentment—right now—and turn it into something positive.

Imagine the possibilities. What would the world look like if people stopped trying to control and manipulate other people; if nations decided to stop controlling other nations? What would happen if relationships were based on "letting go," searching for new life on the ashes of control, manipulation, and power struggles? Simplistic? Perhaps. But, how well has "control" served us in the past?

There's a wonderful line from the musical, "Man of La Mancha", that challenges us to see the world in new ways. "When life seems lunatic," says Don Quixote, "who knows where madness lies? Too much sanity may be madness and, perhaps, to be practical may be the maddest of all. But, the most mad is to see life as it is, and not as it ought to be."

For too long we've seen "control" as the way of the world; the practical, sensible path to take. But, genuine faith challenges us to "let go" and search for the world "as it ought to be."

A Time for Reflection:

How do you relate to the word "control?" How has it affected your life? What's the dark side of that word for you? What's the bright side?

Read this week's scripture lesson several times with great care. What do you think is Paul's message for Christian living?

Have there been times in your life when you've hung tenaciously onto a resentment, absolutely refusing to let it go? How did this affect you (and others)? How did you resolve this situation?

Are there times when "letting go" is, in fact, just plain laziness or cowardice? How do we know when "letting go" is faithful?

"Letting go" naturally creates a void in our lives. What do you think God does when he/she sees a void in us?

"When life seems lunatic, who knows where madness lies? Too much sanity may be madness and, perhaps, to be practical may be the maddest of all. But, the most mad is to see life as it is, and not as it should be." How does this passage affect you? Do you think Don Quixote has found the truth or is he just delusional beyond all common sense?

A Time for Prayer:

Loving God, open us to the great discipline, the wonderful gift of letting go of our resentments, dislikes, and biases and letting you energize us for creative new life. Gracious God, help us understand that our lives aren't intended to have meaning for what we own and control; we aren't loved because we have power. We are loved because you are God and life itself is an exploration of the infinite possibilities we find in your heart. When *you* have control, God, we have abundant life. Your name be praised. Amen.

A Time for Action:

Spend some quiet time with God. Ask him/her about your angers and resentments; all the things you're afraid to release out of your control. In the presence of God decide what you can let go of today. Decide what will take more time to release, even though you're committed to letting it go. What has God given you to fill the void of what you've let go? Act accordingly in the world.

Week 26: Our Welcoming Ways

Criticism is a dime a dozen in our society. It's particularly abundant when it comes to our ability to whine about our own country. Depending on who you talk to and what you read, Canada is either a land of lazy, unproductive hewers of wood and drawers of water that is soon to become an economic backwater or it's a high-tech, high-octane energy leader that's hell-bent on destroying the global environment. Our politicians can't be trusted (we're just a clone of the U.S. anyway). Our medical system is a mess. Our schools are underfunded, our taxes are too high, and you can't drink the water.

It's easy to engage in hyberbolic rants about our country. It's something of a national sport and some rants clearly have the ring of truth to them, if not the whole truth. But, there are times when the rants drain our energy away. There are times when we need to take all the criticism, shake it up, and put it in a beautiful glass container called Canada that carries the shape of peace, justice, freedom, and opportunity, and offers honest welcome to the stranger in our midst. There is surely a time to critique. But, there is also a time to sing loving songs of praise and give thanks for Canada.

"...Come you that are blessed by my Father...for I was hungry and you gave me food, I was thirsty and you gave me something to drink, I was a stranger and you welcomed me, I was naked and

you gave me clothing, I was sick and you took care of me, I was in prison and you visited me..." (Matthew 25: 34-36)

A Personal Journey:

I was an immigrant. I came to Canada in 1971 after having a fundamental disagreement with my home country. In 1977, I experienced one of the proudest moments of my life when I became a Canadian citizen at a very joyful ceremony in Regina, Saskatchewan.

The truth is, jaded as I am, wallowing in the advanced stages of middle age, I can still stick my chest out every day and say that I love this country and I'm proud to be a Canadian.

Canada Day gives me one more chance to celebrate this country. It also provides an opportunity to think, once again, about why I'm celebrating.

When I came to Canada, I didn't know what to expect. I felt lost and alone. I had pretty much abandoned, and been abandoned by, my past. What kind of reception would I get in this vast country that I knew in part, but not very well? Would there be hostility towards me for my choices? Worse, would there be indifference—people just shrugging their shoulders and turning away?

The reason I love this country is that it welcomed me, a stranger, into its midst. I was invited to become part of something new; an exciting, dynamic mix of cultures working together to live well and justly in the world. It was like being invited into a great experiment: "We're not too sure how all this is going to turn out, but you're more than welcome to join us."

This Canada of 1971 jived very nicely with my faith understanding of what life should be and how people should be treated. Most of the world's major faiths place a special emphasis on welcoming the stranger in their midst. It's fundamental to human decency and human progress. My own Christian faith says, "…Come you that are blessed by my Father…for I was hungry and you gave me food, I was thirsty and you gave me something to drink, I was a stranger and you welcomed me, I was naked and you gave me clothing, I was sick and you took care of me, I was in prison and you visited me… (Matthew 25: 34-36)."

I found this spirit in Canada and I fell in love with my new country. It's what I celebrate on Canada Day.

Is Canada perfect? I've lived here for 35 years and I know it's not. Racism, sexism, and ageism have reared their ugly heads throughout our history and continue to dog us today. There have been countless boils and smudges on the body politic that can only be described as shameful. Diverse cultures sometimes fail to find the common ground we need to live together.

I don't celebrate Canada because it's perfect. I celebrate Canada because the core spirit of what I felt back in 1971 still exists today. There is a fundamental decency among the diverse populations that live in our country. The vast majority of us want to live well and justly in the world. The vast majority of us would feel much less excited about the great experiment of Canada if we somehow lost our national spirit and our national courage and stopped welcoming the stranger in our midst. I think we understand what a great loss that would be.

These are trying times. There are some who would have us turn our backs and exclude the stranger. There are some who would teach us to fear the stranger in the names of safety and security. There are some who would have us close the door on the great Canadian experiment.

Those people are wrong. We can't be who we are if we refuse to welcome the stranger in our midst. Our country is lost if we choose safety and security over the values that bind us together in human progress.

Personally, I don't think our country will be lost. Not at all. Too many people have sacrificed too much for us to surrender our core values, the core spirit that makes our country what it is. I love this country. I've loved it ever since I stumbled into Toronto in 1971 with little more than the clothes on my back. I plan on loving it for as long as I live.

A Time for Reflection:

Talk about your "journey" as a Canadian. What has this country done to shape the way you live in the world?

What, in your view, are the core values of Canadian society? Why are they important?

What, in your view, are some ideas or values that threaten our way of life?

What do you think would happen to Canada if we stopped welcoming "the stranger in our midst?" How would that impact our society? How would it impact your faith?

How should Canada deal with the safety and security threats we feel, related to global terrorism?

As Canada Day approaches, how would you finish this sentence: Thank you, Canada, for...?

A Time for Prayer:

Loving God, give us the strength, courage, and wisdom to genuinely welcome the stranger in our midst. Wherever the newcomer is not treated with justice, dignity, and decency in our community give us the voice to speak up. Wherever the newcomer is denied the opportunity for peace, hope, and prosperity give us the grace to stand with them and be a force for change. Welcoming God, teach us what it means to be a welcoming people. Amen.

A Time for Action:

Spend some time volunteering at a new immigrant support centre in your area. Discover the issues affecting newcomers to Canada and share your perspective with your Member of Parliament. Attend a Canada Day celebration and take a quiet moment to finish the sentence: Thank you, Canada, for...

Week 27: The Pilot's Joy

Where does real down-to-earth, bred-in-the-bones joyfulness come from? As a people of faith, we know that there is no real joy unless we feel close to our God. And service to God and God's world is one of the pillars of that closeness, a primary tenet of our faith.

Two professors were discussing what God requires of us in order to be effective and loving servants. One said that a genuine servant of God's world must have a warm heart in order to reach out. You must start with empathy—with a sympathetic, loving connection to people—or you will tire quickly in your service. The second professor disagreed. He said it's not about starting with a warm heart. It's about starting with "a fire in your belly." When you have a fire in your belly, he added, it will warm your heart. In other words, the starting point for God's servants isn't so much about feeling the warmth of God's love in our hearts as it's about feeling a passion for justice in God's name.

The discussion, as you can imagine, will always remain unresolved. Does God's love move you to feeling a passion for justice, or does a passion for justice lead you closer to feeling and understanding God's love? The question for every Christian is this: How do I find true joy as a servant of the Lord?

Make a joyful noise to the Lord, all the earth. Worship the Lord with gladness; come into his presence with singing. Know that the Lord is God. It is he that made us, and we are his; we are his people and the sheep of his pasture. Enter his gates with thanksgiving and his courts with praise. Give thanks to him, bless his name. For the Lord is good; his steadfast love endures forever, and his faithfulness to all generations. (Psalm 100)

A Personal Journey:

Back in the mid-1980s, when I was a young journalist visiting eastern Africa, I had the opportunity to fly with a group known as the Mission Aviation Fellowship (MAF). I have to confess, I wasn't familiar with MAF at the time so I didn't know what to expect as my co-worker and I boarded a little five-seater airplane in Dodoma, Tanzania bound for the tiny lakeside village of Liuli to visit some Canadian development workers.

The flight was one of the most exciting I've ever experienced. The pilot, who'd never been to Liuli before, had several maps spread out on his lap as he followed railway tracks, rivers, and other landmarks until he reached the lake. It was only as we approached the little village that we passengers realized Liuli didn't have a landing strip. Silently, with total concentration, our pilot took the plane down, cruising just a few feet above a patch of land to check for rocks and warn away grazing livestock and playing children. He went up again, made a big arching turn, and executed a perfect landing. Back in those days I didn't have the good sense to be terrified, but I do remember being very thankful when my feet finally touched the ground.

The flight was memorable on many levels. I'd never been in a plane that small. I'd never experienced seat-of-the-pants flying before, and certainly not in Africa. But, one thing that really stood out for me was the attitude of the pilot. Sure, he was confident and highly competent. But, there was more. He exuded a genuine joy for what he was doing. This man loved his job more than anyone I'd met before—or since.

MAF is a faith-based aviation ministry that will this year provide transportation and communication support to over 800 local churches, faith-based ministries, and relief and development organizations in over 30 developing countries worldwide. Back in 1985 our pilot was part of a ministry that today includes a staff of 450 mission families and 130 small planes. Throughout the world, MAF planes take off or land every three minutes, ferrying doctors, missionaries, church leaders, aid workers, and critical supplies to some 2,000 isolated airstrips around the world.

The good work MAF has accomplished in the world since it started flying in 1946 was certainly enough reason in the mid-1980s for our pilot to feel contented and satisfied. But, he wasn't just contented and satisfied with his work, he was joyful.

Why was he joyful? Why was he joyful in his work while most of us are not? Intrepid journalist that I am, I went to the MAF website here in Canada **www.mafc.org** (MAF has head offices in eight countries) and I looked for the "joy," because, frankly, why should they be the only ones who have it?

What I saw on the website was a vital message about the heart of God and the nature of joy. It's not so much that MAF is called "The Wings of Love." It's not even that their mission is "to bring the gospel of God's love in a tangible way." What I noticed was one of their key standards for recruiting new staff. "Above all," according to the standard, "it takes a servant heart first."

Above all, it takes a servant heart first.

I think, more and more, we're getting away from seeing God as a source of sheer, unbridled joy in our world. He/she is more of a fixer. God is called in, like Mike Holmes, to make the best of a bad situation, to give us the strength (sigh) to go on one more day. And, there's no question God's a good fixer with lots of strength to give us. But, where's the joy in our images of the Divine?

It seems to me God wants more than just "OK" for us. God wants joy.

Obviously, we can't all have jobs flying for MAF, so where's our joy going to come from? Maybe it's not the pilot's job we're after, it's his attitude. It's his strength. It's his faith.

God wants us to live with joy. That's a given. So how do we get there? As with all things concerning our faith, we get there by searching the Word. Joy is held up in the Bible for everyone to see. And, its essence is distilled by MAF in their search for new staff: "Above all, it takes a servant heart first." The fact is, there's no joy in a world that's only about "me." Reaching out to help another is reaching out to touch God and that's where joy is found.

A Time for Reflection:

Re-read the introduction to this week's devotion, taking note of the professors' different ideas on where the starting point for true servanthood should be. What's the starting point, the primary motivation, for your servanthood in the world?

We all live in the world with differing physical, mental, and emotional capacities. What does it mean to you when it's said that every person of faith is called to be a servant of God?

What does it mean to you to call God a "fixer?" How do you feel about the Divine image of "God the fixer?"

Is God a joyful figure for you? Why or why not? Where does your image of God come from?

Meditate for a moment and create a mental picture of where joy actually comes from in your life. Where do you see God in that picture?

"Above all, it takes a servant heart first." What do you think that means for the pilots who fly for MAF? What does it mean for you in your day to day life?

A Time for Prayer:

Gracious God, thank you for the gift of servanthood. Help us to use our talents and skills to be sensitive, persistent, and committed helpers in your world. Open us to the joy of breaking away from the constant, diligent pursuit of self-satisfaction in order to reach out to others and find you in the smile of our neighbours and their new songs of hope. Guide us to move in our lives from selfishness to self-giving. We pray in Christ's name. Amen.

A Time for Action:

Take some time to spend with God. Perhaps it's a few hours, a few days, or a few weeks. Ask God to show you how you can turn your life from self-involvement to servanthood. What aspects of your current lifestyle can you turn into the positive service of God's world? What attitudes does God want you to transform in order to live with the joy of a kingdom servant? When God shows you the way (however God shows you the way), follow it.

Dean Salter

Week 28: Let the Sun Shine In

There's little question that Job is one of the most put-upon characters in the Bible. This poor man loses virtually everything he counts on in life: family, wealth, home, health, and position. Reading through the Book of Job is like thumbing the pages of the worst horror story you can imagine. Poor Job. Who wouldn't blurt out anguished cries of 'why me?' in the face of such unmitigated agony?

It takes a while to find anything positive in the Book of Job. But, when it comes it's very important. It comes when God, "out of the whirlwind," answers Job's devastated rants. The very fact God chooses to respond tells us that God is a personal God who cares for his/her creation. Why respond if Job doesn't matter? The response itself tells us, while we may not always understand it, there is nevertheless divine order and divine justice for all creation. What has been created has been created with care. What has been created is good and will never be abandoned by God.

In the last analysis, we were not there when God laid the foundation of the earth. But, we live with great confidence that when it happened "all the heavenly beings shouted for joy."

Then the Lord answered Job out of the whirlwind: "Who is this that darkens counsel by words without knowledge? Gird up your loins like a man, I will question you, and you shall declare to me. Where

*were you when I laid the foundation of the earth?
Tell me, if you have understanding. Who determined
its measurements—surely you know! Or who
stretched the line upon it? On what were its bases
sunk, or who laid its cornerstone when the
morning stars sang together and all the heavenly
beings shouted for joy?*
(Job 38: 1-7)

A Personal Journey:

My office is a mess.

Six months ago I started working at home and,
initially, I had definite plans to keep my workspace
neat. Within a day or two, papers began to pile up and,
well, they just never stopped. Today, it's reached the
point where books, files, and documents litter the
floor like giant mushrooms and I've decided that
neatness is highly overrated.

I think this burgeoning mess is the reason I never
realized that there are two "suns" sitting on my desk.
And, they're as different as two suns can be. The first
is pictured in an old Ziggy cartoon that's pinned into a
battered silver frame. Ziggy is just opening his window
shade to see what kind of a day it is. The window is
almost filled with the morning sun, which is sticking
out a big red tongue at him. The caption says, "Try to
have a nice day." At one time, this obviously appealed
to my twisted sense of humour.

Two feet away from Ziggy's encounter with the sun,
there's another sun that was drawn by my daughter
many, many years ago. It's a huge, golden sun painted
on cardboard with a wide, toothy smile and brilliant
red and gold "rays" emanating from the circle in all
directions. The message written below this carefully
crafted sun is: "Happy Father's Day, Dad."

It occurred to me as I stared at the two "suns" the
other day that I spend far too much of my time living

under Ziggy's sun, listening for the sour notes, cynically hoping for the best but expecting the worst each day. It's easy to believe that Ziggy's sun is "realistic"—that it's the way of the world.

One day last week I was running around trying to "do business" and I managed to run into virtually every road construction project in the city. That's a lot of projects, and a lot of waiting. Ziggy's sun told me, as the frustration rose, that this must be some cosmic plot to throw me off—to ruin my day. Oh, the humanity! How can bad things happen to such good people? The more projects I ran into the more I boiled. I couldn't imagine these projects had some positive aim. They were just a pain! Ziggy's sun.

But, you know, Ziggy's sun isn't good enough. I want to live in a world where it makes eminent good sense to fix the roads—where the positives of life hold all the power. All things considered, I want to make more time and find more ways to live under my daughter's brilliant, friendly sun.

I look at that sun and I see a world of possibilities, an open world that celebrates the best gifts we have to offer. I see hope and acceptance in that ridiculously wide smile. I see laughter in those welcoming eyes. In my daughter's sun, there is nothing arrayed against me; no forces of evil, no slippery slope into bad luck and failure. My daughter's sun vibrates with the colours of life and hope. You can dream dreams with that picture. You can fail and still find the courage to believe in your success.

I'm not going to clean up my office anytime soon. O.K., probably never. But, I'm going to find a prominent place for my daughter's picture. In her own way, she has offered a bright golden window onto a life well-lived.

A Time for Reflection:

We all face hardships in our lives; some of us more than others. It's unlikely any of us will live our lives without experiencing pain and loss. How did you feel and how did you react to a particularly painful event in your life at the time it happened?

What did you need to believe about God in order to help you during your hardship? What did you need to believe about the people around you? About yourself?

How much of your life do you spend under Ziggy's sun with the "forces of evil" arrayed against you? Why do you spend time there?

How much of your life do you spend under "the daughter's sun?" What do you need to know; what do you have to feel and do in order to live under that sun?

As a person of faith, what is "success" for you and what is "failure?" Who is God for you as you live your way through the hardships and joys of life?

A Time for Prayer:

Gracious God, help us live in the firm confidence that you are God even in the midst of our greatest pain and our deepest losses. Help us to understand in our hearts that your caring for creation is unshakable, that your love is steadfast and healing, that your justice is real, and that you created the world with such majesty that "all the heavenly beings shouted for joy." Guide us to believe in your grace, even when the houses we've built begin to crumble around us. Amen.

A Time for Action:

Spend some time with God, talking about which of the two suns described above is most powerful in your life. Reflect and pray each day about your "encounters" and "interactions" with the world. Where did you let God in and where did you try to hold him/her at arm's length? How strongly did the sun shine for you? With God's help, begin to shift more and more of your time and energy into living under "the daughter's sun."

Week 29: The Big Picture

There are times in our lives when things go along quite nicely. The winds are at our backs, the messages bouncing around in our heads are positive, and our social environment puts a smile on our faces. It's good to see God in our happiness. But, there are other times when a little upstart voice creates some doubt in our minds. The little voice asks if what we're doing is who we are. It wants to know if we're living the big picture of our lives, using the gifts we've been given, or quietly hiding our life-lights where they can't be seen. There's a good chance that this annoying, persistent, and complicated little voice is the voice of God for us. How are we supposed to respond when God challenges us with the big picture, particularly when our lives seem to revolve around countless little ones?

"No one after lighting a lamp hides it under a jar, or puts it under a bed, but puts it on a lampstand, so that those who enter may see the light. For nothing is hidden that will not be disclosed , nor is anything secret that will not become known and come to light. Then pay attention to how you listen; for to those who have, more will be given; and from those who do not have, even what they seem to have will be taken away." (Luke 8: 16-18)

A Personal Journey:

I battled my way into Toronto the other day—two hours of stop and go driving on the 401 highway—to do an interview for a magazine article. I'd been asked to write a profile of P.V. and Annie Chandy, who had just returned to Canada after 19 years of missionary service in the struggling Asian country of Nepal. By the time I found their apartment in the wilds of east-end Toronto, I was frazzled by all the roadwork that had slowed my way. "Six months of winter and six months of construction," I angrily mumbled to myself as I finally reached their door a half hour late.

Within a few minutes this talented, unassuming couple turned my over-heated, self-involved day around as they told their story.

By contemporary standards, the Chandys had the world by the tail in Edmonton back in the 1980s. P.V. and Annie had good jobs, good friends, a beautiful young family, and a brand new custom-built house. Their future looked as bright as the wall-to-wall prairie sky. But, in their hearts, they knew something was missing. "We had that feeling," they told me, "that we were losing the big picture."

That "feeling" led them to sign on as "overseas personnel" with The United Church of Canada and spend two years as teachers in a remote mountain village in Nepal. The experience spurred them on to another 17 years serving the country in education, administration, and medicine. They made an enormous contribution and they wouldn't have traded the experience for anything.

At the close of the interview, all I could think of was "the big picture." What is "the big picture" anyway? Surely not everyone needs to drop everything and head to Nepal in order to live out "the big picture" for their lives. Most of us wouldn't last two seconds under a thatched roof, three day's walk from the nearest town.

I'd like to take a stab at this "big picture" thing. At the risk of trotting out old doctrines—well—let me trot out an old doctrine. In the United Church Creed it says, "We live in God's world." It strikes me that this just might be "the big picture" in a nutshell. In God's world, we're called out of our self-image and beyond our self-doubts. We're asked to see a world of communities, created and loved by God. We're asked to understand and live out a positive role in the wider world of God's family.

"We live in God's world." It doesn't mean we ignore the self. It does mean our lives are more than self-indulgence. The "big picture," I think, is the realization that we're not isolated and alone, tiny specks on a bottomless, boundless sea. We're part of a community, called to be connected with one another as both gift givers and gift receivers.

I'm not going to Nepal anytime soon. And neither are you, probably. It's not our "big picture." But on these lush summer days, it's valuable to find a shady spot somewhere to think about what "the big picture" really is for you. If this is, indeed, God's world, where are you connected to it? What are you called to give? What are you being offered?

Maybe you need a new relationship with family and friends. Maybe that's "the big picture." Or maybe there's a piece of work in the community that's calling your name. Maybe, like the Chandys, there's a part of the world somewhere that's crying out for what you can give. Who knows what the "little voice" is saying, or what it'll say in the future? Who knows what picture will be painted in your mind?

The Chandys are a very courageous couple. They placed themselves in God's hands and listened for "the big picture" of what it meant for them to live in God's world back in the 1980s. Soon enough, God painted a picture that forever changed their lives and countless other lives on the far side of the planet. To live in God's world is to believe, to have faith, that God will paint a "big picture" for each of us. It's also a commitment to divest of some "old pictures" in order to frame something new.

A Time for Reflection:

Where is your life-light right now? Is it shining on top of the table or hidden below it? Where are you right now in the "happiness-challenge" dialogue with God?

What would you say are the God-given gifts which you can bring to relationships and to the community?

How do you exercise these gifts right now? Where are you connected to God's world?

What, at this point in time, do you think God's big picture is for you?

What do you think the big picture might become in the future as you listen to the "little voice" of God in your life?

What stands in the way of your ability to successfully live out your "big picture?"

A Time for Prayer:

Loving God, over and over we thank you for the skills and talents with which you've gifted us. You have given us wonderful opportunities in this world. But, over and over we must confess that we're afraid to use our gifts. We squander them in self-pity or self-indulgence and lack the faith to be the people you call us to be. Forgive us, God. Guide us to listen to your voice, honour your gracious gifts, and make a firm commitment to live the big picture of our lives. Amen.

A Time for Action:

Go and find a shady spot. Feel the presence of God. Open your mind and heart to all the possibilities of life. Listen for the "little voice" of guidance. Discuss with it, argue with it if you have to, but respect its power in your life. When you're ready, write down on a piece of paper what "the big picture" for your life is at this point in time as a person of faith. Discuss your "big picture" with family and trusted friends and move at your own pace towards accomplishing the life God has set out for you.

Week 30: How Do You Know If You're Having a Good Holiday?

While the great challenges of life involve leading a "servant life" and reaching out to God's world in love, there is also a time to step back and engage in prayer and reflection. In short, in order to be authentic and effective in our servanthood, we need to take some "me" time to check the foundations and pillars that support who we are as people. There are many well-meaning people who run wildly about, trying to "do good" through membership in countless committees, groups, and societies. Their briefcases are overflowing with papers they have no time to read; their contributions are often stilted and irrelevant. Good-spirited as they may be, these people are ineffective because they're unfocused. They haven't taken any "me" time for prayer and reflection. They're not grounded in what God is actually calling them to do and be. They don't take time to understand the authentic nature of their own servanthood.

"Ask, and it will be given you; search, and you will find; knock, and the door will be opened for you. For everyone who asks receives, and everyone who searches finds, and for everyone who knocks the door will be opened. Is there anyone among you who, if your child asks for bread, will give a stone? Or if the child asks for a fish, will give a snake? If you then, who are evil, know how to give good gifts to your children, how much more will

your Father in heaven give good things to those who ask him!"
(Matthew 7: 7-11)

A Personal Journey:

Over the last few years I've been doing a lot of editorial work for various writer-experts who are always producing new articles on the top 10 ways to get the results you want in your local church.

There always seem to be exactly 10 steps that'll get people excited about a fundraising campaign or 10 steps your group can use to bring off a new building project. Through some cosmic coincidence there never seem to be nine or 11 steps, always 10. Follow them to a "T" and you've got it made.

Well, I've decided to join the fray—sort of. Given the fact we're now cruising through summer, I've decided to suggest "The Top Five Indicators You're Having a Good Holiday." If I was a true expert on this subject, you'd get 10 indicators. But, the best I can do right now is five. I've cleverly instituted a point system to divert you from thinking about the fact I'm five indicators short.

The Top Five Indicators You're Having a Good Holiday

You know you're having a good holiday if you've read a book all the way through in less than a week. Give yourself one point for this. If you've bought a book for the holidays but can't remember its name or where you put it, subtract one point.

You know you're having a good holiday if you've been able to have calm, insightful conversations with your spouse and your children, learning new things about their lives and interests. Give yourself one point for this. If you can't find your spouse or your children because they're avoiding you like the plague, subtract one point.

You know you're having a good holiday if you've felt a sense of joy in the natural world around you, or if you've learned something exciting about the natural world and it has opened up some spiritual insight about *your place* in the universe. Give yourself one point for this. If you're wondering why you're missing Canadian Idol to fight a bitter, losing battle with blackflies, mosquitoes, and damp firewood, subtract one point.

You know you're having a good holiday if it gives you a chance to calmly reflect on why you live, work, and volunteer your time the way you do; if it gives you a chance to reflect on your old and new dreams for yourself—and share this with others. Give yourself one point for this. If you're on the beach every day waiting for your cellphone to ring so you can iron out thorny problems at work, subtract one point.

You know you're having a good holiday if you feel refreshed and thankful for the time off and, at the end, you're ready to rejoin your day-to-day life back home. Give yourself one point for this. If you need a week to recover from your holiday, subtract one point.

If you find yourself four or five points on the plus side, I'd say you're having a pretty successful holiday. If you're four or five points on the negative side, I'd say you're not having a holiday so much as you're having a painful "episode."

There have been a few summers when I would've been reluctant to add up these numbers myself. I'm sure we've all had some painful holiday experiences.

But, isn't it amazing when we can allow holidays to do what they're supposed to do: refresh and renew us; put us back in touch with the people, thoughts, and dreams that give us life and purpose throughout the year?

What a pleasure it is to say, "Now that was a good holiday," and actually mean it— because Dean Salter's brilliant five-step analysis never lies.

A Time for Reflection:

From your perspective is "me" time important or is it overrated? Why do you feel that way?

Life often pulls us in many different directions. How do you focus on what you are "called" to do in your world? Is there a way of ensuring that who you are and what you do reflects the foundation and pillars at the core of your life?

What are the goals you set for your holidays? Do you build in any time for reflection, quiet interaction with family, and general self-care? Do you feel refreshed when your holiday is over?

What role does prayer play in your self-care? How do you pray and how does it make you feel? Do you think prayer could play a bigger role in your life?

Re-read this week's scripture. Does God give us what we ask for, help us find what we want, and open all the doors we want opened? Take some time to reflect on who God is for you and what God's kingdom is all about according to your beliefs.

A Time for Prayer:

Loving God, help us to meet you in the quiet spaces of our lives as well as in the rush of daily events. Guide us to take serious and authentic time to reflect on the holiness with which we're surrounded in life. Empower us to touch the foundation of our own lives and to feel the strong pillars that give us proof of who we are. Gracious God, we pray for the courage and strength to be quiet in the face of life's many demands and know that you are God, the author of every good and perfect gift. Amen.

A Time for Action:

Use the five-part holiday analysis above as a way of reflecting on your last holiday. Plan your next holiday so that you have a good chance of coming out with a "plus five" rating and a positive sense that you've touched the foundation and pillars of your life and felt refreshed and renewed.

Week 31: There's No Sign of God Up Here

With all the talk about God in our world today it's surprising that so little light is shone on who (or what) God actually is. Most Sunday School versions of God paint the picture of a white-haired, Rubenesque man who lolls around in a physical place called "heaven" making what must amount to trillions of decisions each second specifically affecting individual lives. This very busy man must orchestrate everything from answering prayers to the distribution of natural disasters.

Historically, theologians have worked diligently to muddy the Sunday School waters by referring to God as "the wholly other" and encouraging the faithful to understand God as a "spiritual being" rather than a human being. Given the tenuous connection between the Sunday School God and reality as we know it, theologians have properly introduced us to the wonderful world of metaphor and symbol. All of which has made life and faith much more authentic for the more liberal-minded faithful, but also much more difficult.

It's one thing to consult the scriptures and generate a long list of God's likes and dislikes. It's another to have a cogent belief in who or what God actually is for us right now and how we connect with he, she, or it in our daily lives. How do we know God is speaking to us if we have no sense of who or what God is?

In the beginning was the Word, and the Word was with God, and the Word was God. He was in the beginning with God. All things came into being through him, and without him not one thing came into being. What has come into being in him was life, and the life was the light of all people. The light shines in the darkness, and the darkness did not overcome it. (John 1: 1-5)

A Personal Journey:

One of the more profound theological statements of the last century came from a very unlikely source.

Some 45 years ago, when the first Soviet cosmonauts began to orbit the earth, one of their number was good enough to look out his spacecraft windows in all directions and pronounce, "There's no sign of God up here."

At the time, this caused quite a stir among believers who were appalled at the impertinence of this godless Communist. For many, whose God was captured perfectly on the ceiling of the Sistine Chapel, the cosmonaut was either lying through his teeth or the spacecraft was simply in the wrong orbit to see God floating around.

While the observation ignited a firestorm of indignation, the whole kerfuffle actually passed away fairly quickly. Which is too bad, because the cosmonaut was right. God wasn't "up there" in space, certainly not in the form many people expected the Divine to take. To this day, the Sistine Chapel God hasn't been sighted in outer space.

If we'd taken the godless Communists a little more seriously (or if they were slightly less aggravating) we might have taken the opportunity to expand our images of God. If God isn't a human-shaped creature floating happily in the cosmos, then what?

Recently, we were at a very nice cottage on Oxtongue Lake, near Algonquin Park in Ontario. The first night of our visit I ventured out onto the dock to commune with nature. I was hoping to experience the Divine in some new way as darkness settled over the inky black water and the thickly forested hills.

As I searched the heavens for a "sign" and waited for some "experience" of God, I was swarmed by a wave of mosquitoes so massive that I felt little needles all over my body and I raced back to the cottage as fast as I could run. God would not be available tonight!

The next day, I sat on the beach in brilliant sunshine. The water sparkled as if it was filled with millions of diamonds. Now I'm going to experience the Divine, I thought. Now I'm going to gain some new wisdom, some new insight. But, within minutes, the deer flies began circling. Little stealth bombers capable of severing limbs, I had to be careful of them. So I spent the entire day waving my hands crazily over my head, which, to a deer fly, apparently means "let's play." Once again, God was not available.

I went home disappointed. Like the cosmonauts, I concluded that "God was not up there."

Just the other day, back home again, I was walking in my neighbourhood when I saw a little three-year-old trailing after her mother along the opposite sidewalk. The little one was obviously tired and bedraggled with the heat. Very gently, the mother turned, swept the little girl up in her arms, gave her a kiss, and said, "It's lemonade time!"

And the little girl smiled a smile that lit up the neighbourhood. It dawned on me that God was in that little scene. I couldn't manufacture the moment. I couldn't order up the image. It just was. Not "up there," but "here." And there wasn't a mosquito or a deer fly in sight.

A Time for Reflection:

Discuss your first images of God. What were they and where did they come from? How did these images make you feel about the world?

Has your image of God changed over the years? If so, what brought about this change? As a person of faith, how do you see God today? Describe what you see, or what you think of, when you say the word "God" as a believer.

Do you think it's important for people to share the same image and understanding of God? Why or why not?

Are there specific things about the nature of God that people need to share in common? List some of those things.

The Soviet cosmonauts shook many people's faith when they declared that there was no evidence of God in "the heavens." Given your own image of God, is there anything that would shake your faith today?

Is a "shaken image" of God always a bad thing? Do you think your current image of God is open to change?

A Time for Prayer:

Loving God, grant us the courage to search for you in the high and low moments of our lives. Give us eyes to see you in unexpected places. Give us ears to hear you in words we've tried to ignore. Give us voice to speak to you, even when we doubt your presence. Gracious God, give us the wisdom to break through our stereotypes and biases and experience you in growing circles of awareness as well as in the timeless constancy of your love. Amen.

A Time for Action:

Organize or join a study group consisting of people who want to focus time and prayer on the image and nature of God for them. If it's helpful, choose a book to study which offers a challenging perspective on "who God is" for people of faith. Consider how images of God affect how people live and act in the world.

Week 32: Taking Resurrection Out of the Clouds

The traditional concept of resurrection is a little hard for most liberal-minded Christians to swallow. As depicted in a host of "B" movies, a ghost-like form of the dead person climbs out of its fleshy clone and ascends up to heaven, hanging out in the clouds, and carrying on some kind of "afterlife" that appears so excruciatingly boring that the ghostly apparition must surely wish they were dead. But, of course, they *are* dead, and apparently forever doomed to a vapid afterlife of idle cloud-sitting. Given the hellishness of heaven, you might wish you could give resurrection a "pass" and just stay non-existent.

But, resurrection doesn't belong in the clouds. That's the main point of this week's devotion. We need to rescue it from the realm of the bizarre and find it again in the cut and thrust of daily life. When and where is God offering us resurrection in this world? What choices can we make that move our spirits closer to the heart of God?

Jesus said to her (Martha), "I am the resurrection and the life. Those who believe in me, even though they die, will live, and everyone who lives and believes in me will never die. Do you believe this?" She said to him, "Yes, Lord, I believe that you are the Messiah, the Son of God, the one coming into the world." (John 11: 25-27)

A Personal Journey:

There was a man—let's call him John—who was living an unexceptional life somewhere between the boundaries of rich and poor, happy and sad. He had a home, a family, a few friends, and a decent job. If you asked him, he would describe the day to day flow of his life as being "OK." Not brilliant by any means, but "OK."

Then, in the span of a few weeks, his world started to unravel. He lost his job. His relationship with his wife, strained at the best of times, became worse and they separated. John moved into a small basement apartment with peeling paint and few furnishings. His tiny array of "friends" avoided him. Two weeks after moving out, John learned that his mother, a solid rock in his life, had been diagnosed with a radical cancer and she wasn't expected to live for more than a few weeks.

John spent most of his time in his cold, dark apartment. He could feel his eyes constantly welling with tears. He couldn't sleep. He had no energy—not even to shave and brush his teeth. His shrinking world seemed filled with a sense of helplessness and hopelessness. When he thought of anything, the words of his abusive father arrived like unwelcome guests. "What's the matter with you, John? Can't you do anything right? I can't imagine how you'll ever amount to anything in this world."

Finally, on a bright, warm summer day, John reached the far end of his strength. He couldn't go on any longer. He drove his car to the edge of a familiar cliff that dropped 100 feet into the powerful river he'd known since he was a boy. He walked to the edge and stared at the abyss. But some unnamed force within him wouldn't allow him to let go; wouldn't allow him to take the last step of his life.

He didn't know it or understand it at the time, but this was his moment of resurrection. This was the key moment when he chose life over death. He stepped back and, in that moment, he began a new journey.

It isn't as if John's life changed overnight. He still faced the same pain, the same sense of loss as before. But, he faced it as a man who had stepped back from the brink; as a man who had chosen life over death.

John would never be rich or powerful, or even wildly popular, but he would be a man who had strangely...mysteriously... felt resurrection in the deepest part of his soul. John chose life. There's no question that his life journey would hold pain for John, but it would also hold joy.

We may think that resurrection is a rather strange, rather antiquated concept that we can cover off with a few good hymns and some time-worn scripture passages back at Easter. But, resurrection is more than that. It's about John. It's about the spirit that looks death in the face, all forms of death, and turns them into life. It's about that *something* in us (we'll name it "Christ") that calls us back from the brink of death and challenges us with the journey of life.

Our whole notion of resurrection needs to be...well...resurrected. It's not about the past. It's about the present and the future. When we come to know, through the power of Christ, that death is no match for life, our worldview changes dramatically. Our life's journey sings with a new radical hope, a hope which is the child of resurrection.

A Time for Reflection:

Talk about your concept of resurrection. What do you believe about it? What don't you believe about it? Has it brought you strength in your faith or doubt?

How is the concept of resurrection that's presented above different from the traditional images? How do you feel about a "day to day" resurrection?

When and where is God offering us resurrection today? Have you seen resurrection at work in the world? Where would you like to see it at work in the world?

In your daily life, where do you need to find resurrection? Where in your life do you need to open up to God and work to turn death into life?

Does resurrection always turn sadness into joy?

A Time for Prayer:

God of resurrection, in your son Jesus Christ may we find life in the dark shadows of death. In Christ, may we find hope when our life journey spirals into the valley of despair. Gracious God, when we stagger to the precipice and every fibre of our being urges us to take the last steps of self-destruction, we thank you for the possibilities of resurrection. In you there is gain, when all we can see is loss. In you there is hope when we have lost our way. In you there is life even as we stagger to the very edge of death. Help us, God, to reach out and touch your saving hand. Amen.

A Time for Action:

Walk with God and name the "demons" which represent death in your life. Talk with God and discover what resurrection looks like for you. With God's help, how do you turn the deaths of your day to day world into new and vibrant life? How do you give life the victory? Offer the "demons" to God by name and work on them one by one.

Week 33: God's...Good...Creation

This week, let's spend our devotional time focusing on three critical words that mean the world to people of faith: God's...good...creation. To say something belongs to God is a profound statement of faith. To say that the beautiful blue planet Earth belongs to God is a clear statement of how magnificent and valuable it is and of how the earth calls out honour, respect, and love from those of us who are merely gardeners here. The word "good" is a challenge to all of us. Do we dare defile a planet which a caring God has surveyed and called "good?" How do we renew what has already been defiled? Finally, the word "creation," and the knowledge that God "created" the world, tells us that the natural world is a beautiful work of art to be admired and respected, and from which we can gain inspiration. God's canvas should never be hauled down, scratched, and battered.

God's...good...creation. Saying the words is not enough. How do we bring them into the core of our everyday consciousness and turn each word into a lifetime of action?

And God said, "Let the waters under the sky be gathered together into one place, and let the dry land appear." And it was so. God called the dry land Earth, and the waters that were gathered together he called Seas. And God saw that it was good.
(Genesis 1: 9-10)

A Personal Journey:

I tried to make a joke the other day about global warming. I said in a country like Canada, where we often face nine months of winter and three months of hard slogging, why should we complain if the world is getting a little warmer? Is it such a bad thing not to be frozen stiff in January? Maybe Floridians will start trekking north in January to enjoy the balmy temperatures.

It was a pretty weak joke at several different levels. But, it was weak primarily because global warming just isn't funny. It's probably one of the most colossal dangers our planet has ever faced. "Faced" may be the wrong word, since we aren't facing it at all. "Ignored" is probably more to the point.

How bad is the situation? A recent report from the U.S. National Academy of Sciences said that the earth's temperature has reached levels not seen in thousands of years. The earth has been warming at a rate of 0.2 degrees Celsius per decade over the last three decades, with strong warming in the far north and significant warming of the western Pacific and Indian oceans. These two oceans have a major effect on climate and their warming could lead to dramatic global weather changes. If the earth continues to warm, the polar ice caps will continue to melt, leading inexorably to coastal flooding on a massive scale. In addition to the disastrous flooding of coastal cities and towns, climate change has the potential to cause incalculable damage to the farming, fishing, and forestry sectors worldwide as soil and water conditions are altered by the weather.

Global warming, caused by man-made pollution such as vehicle emissions and industrial gases, is reaching dangerous levels, according to NASA scientist James Hansen. Hansen led the global warming study team which developed the National Academy of Sciences report. Commenting on the report, Hansen said, "If further global warming reaches two or three degrees Celsius, we will likely see changes that make earth a different planet than the one we know. The last time it was that warm was in the middle of the Pliocene, about three million years ago, when sea level was estimated to have been about 25 metres higher than today."

One of the most shocking realities is that governments, particularly in North America, are doing little to address the problem. Recently, Canada's Environment Commissioner Johanne Gelinas issued a report which largely condemned both the past Liberal and the current Conservative governments for doing little to curb the "greenhouse gases" which cause global warming; and for not giving the issue proper attention in future planning. Gelinas noted that greenhouse gases in Canada's oil sector have increased more than 50 percent since 1990 and that Alberta oilsands emissions could double by 2015.

From a faith perspective, the spoiling of the planet by human hands is both an environmental crisis and a crisis of the human spirit—a palpable sin against the very nature of God. In the biblical creation story, God creates the heavens and the earth, day and night, the seas and the sky, plants and animals, and humankind. After each act of creation the scripture says, "And God saw that it was good." After the sixth day the scripture goes a step further and says, "God saw everything that he had made, and indeed, it was very good."

God created the world exactly as he/she chose to create it. Chaos had been brought into order. Everything was designed in a perfect balance. Every element of creation was designed to prosper in the "good" world God had created.

One of the great crises of the human spirit today is that we have chosen to defile God's creation. We've upset the balance. We've taken the order and beauty of our planet—all that God has called "good"—and done our level best to turn it back into chaos. Entire species have become extinct, rivers and oceans are rank with pollution, and the air is dangerous to breathe. Because we've failed to manage our work on this planet the earth is warming dangerously and the goodness is slowly being cooked away.

Is there any good news in this whole story? Perhaps the good news is the fact God has never abandoned us in our spiritual crises. God's strength is there for us. Perhaps the good news is that God's creation is still God's creation and what God has called "good" is still good. In my humble estimation, today God is calling all of us to re-examine what is "good." God is calling us to repentance. God is calling us to have a plan to undo the damage which can still be undone. We are called to battle chaos and restore balance. We have fiercely taken from this planet to the point of devastation. It would be an offence against God not to develop an equally fierce plan for restoration.

A Time for Reflection:

What does it mean to you personally to say (and believe) that we live in God's world? How does it affect what you say and do on a daily basis?

What does it mean to you personally to say that the created world is "good?" Why is it "good" and what does its goodness mean for the way we conduct our lives? What does it mean when we see parts of the world which are clearly not "good?"

What does it mean to you when you see an artist's "creation?" How do you know when such a creation has meaning for you? The world is God's creation. How would you respond to these two questions when thinking about God's creation?

Where have we gone wrong? What is the nature of our sin that we have created such devastation to our environment?

What steps, both simple and complex, do we need to take as individuals and as members of a community in order to help restore the balance of God's good earth? Brainstorm. Make a list.

A Time for Prayer:

Gracious God, forgive us for our greed, pride, and hard-heartedness as we stand in the garden of your good world. You have given us rich earth and pure water and our chemicals have drained their life-giving essence away. You've given us clean air and we've returned it to you choked with pollutants. Guide us, God, into repentance for believing that the world is ours, not yours. Turn us into healers and show us how to stand with the created world as lovers, rather than against it as tormentors and assassins. Reform and renew our spirits, O God we pray. Amen.

A Time for Action:

Go back to the brainstorming and list-making you did in "A Time for Reflection." Pick some doable, measurable steps you can take to help the environment. Make a plan that names your actions and sets out clearly when and how you plan to accomplish your goals and how you'll know if you've succeeded. Once you've made a plan, get started as soon as possible.

Week 34: Star Power

It's hard to be a perfectionist in this world. To try to make everything come out clean, neat, and perfectly ordered; to always excel and come out on the winning side, is a pretty tough place to hang your self-image. Things happen. We aren't always at our best and we don't always get the best breaks in life. The world can be a stubbornly messy place that refuses to conform to our will and "doing the best we can do" is quite a different concept from "achieving perfection." Perhaps the truest test of our humanity and our faith isn't the pursuit of perfection at all. Perhaps it's how we react in the face of adversity, how we deal with our losses.

Yet whatever gains I had, these I have come to regard as loss because of Christ. More than that, I regard everything as loss because of the surpassing value of knowing Christ Jesus my Lord. For his sake I have suffered the loss of all things, and I regard them as rubbish, in order that I may gain Christ... (Philippians 3: 7-8)

A Personal Journey:
It was a summer Sunday in 2004 and I was riveted to our little television set all afternoon. I screamed, I yelled, I groaned, and I looked to the heavens for help and guidance. I did everything I could to help golfer Mike Weir win the Canadian Open. And I wasn't alone. One of the largest television audiences in the history

of the Open and a deafening gallery at the Glen Abbey golf course in Oakville, Ontario hung on his every shot in the final round. Could it really happen? Could the talented Weir be the first Canadian to win our Open since 1954?

Well, the short answer is 'no.' It didn't happen. Weir came maddeningly, outrageously close—an inch away—but it didn't happen. Vijay Singh beat our hero on the third hole of a playoff and left Canadian golf fans with one big collective "sigh" over a lost opportunity to fly *our* flag over *our* event.

If the fans sagged and sighed over Weir's defeat in the 100th Canadian Open, imagine how Mike must have felt. It was his childhood dream to win the Canadian Open. "I can remember," he said, "(dreaming of) being on the putting green and having a putt to win the tournament." He had the putt in 2004, but it missed by an inch.

There are some key moments when sport and day-to-day life cross over one another. In the nexus of that crossing something vital and important happens. There's no question that Mike Weir's golf game shone brightly that summer's day at Glen Abbey. He played brilliantly, like the world-class golfer he is. But, it's important to recognize that his humanity shone just as brightly once the tournament was over.

Character and faith are defined as much by defeat as by victory; as much by loss as by gain. How do we see the world when we lose by an inch? How does the world look when something near and dear to us is taken away in the blink of an eye? It's easy to give up and give out; to be certain that the "principalities and powers" of this world are arrayed against us. It is much harder to keep our heads up and thank God for a world of gift and opportunity. It's hard to taste failure and still find the heart to thank God for a new day and new possibilities. It's hard to own up to our failings, but not be owned by them. It's hard, but it's critical.

Mike Weir didn't blame anybody or anything but himself for his finish at the 2004 Canadian Open. That's character. In an interview following the event, he told his fans that he plans on having a long career; that there's bound to be lots of ups and downs. And, as far as the Canadian Open goes, he said, "I'll be back."

You could tell it wasn't just bravado. It was character and faith, a genuine belief in the bigger world of hope and possibilities. Mike Weir didn't win the 2004 Canadian Open, but he showed us, in his quiet way, what it takes to be a "star" in this world.

A Time for Reflection:

Do you try to "make things perfect" for special events or occasions? What does "perfect" look like for you and how often have you achieved it in your life? How does it make you feel when you fall short of perfection?

What's the difference in your mind between "perfection" and "doing the best you can do" in life? What are you striving for and why?

What do you think of Mike Weir's response to losing the 2004 Canadian Open? How else could he have responded? How would you have responded and why? What are some basic principles to follow in responding to adversity?

Why does Mike Weir's response to adversity make him a "star" in this world? Are there other athlete/celebrity "role models" who are less "stellar" in defeat? What impact do they have on society?

The Apostle Paul tells the church at Philippi that "...whatever gains I had, these I have come to regard as loss because of Christ." What is Paul saying here? What is the perspective he's offering us on what's "important" and "vital" in living our lives as people of faith?

A Time for Prayer:

Loving God, help us to truly understand and open ourselves to the power of Jesus Christ in our lives. Help us to know that whether we have success or failure in the activities and challenges of our day-to-day lives, we are held firmly in the love of Christ and, in him, there is no loss. In him, we have gained the joy of our lives. Amen.

A Time for Action:

Talk with God about what's important for you in your life and faith. Define the top three "challenges" in your life today. Throw out the word "perfection." Address each challenge as someone who has been gifted by God and called to "do your best" in response to the love of Christ.

Week 35: Bringing Our Values to the Workplace

You would think something as profound as a "value" would be chiseled in stone, immutable, and proudly displayed where everyone can see it. We could joyously point to it in every life situation and say, "This is my value." But, we all know that those things we call "values" are often written on chalkboards rather than chiseled in stone. For example, is our value of "honesty" equally noble and honourable in every relationship of our day-to-day lives? Is our honesty at home with family the same honesty that we apply to our workplace, or to a thorny relationship, or to a sticky situation we're trying to extricate ourselves from? Should it be? Is it better for our values to be flexible and situational? Each of us faces a complex, critical question every day our lives: How do we value our values?

Then Pilate entered the headquarters again, summoned Jesus and asked him, "Are you the King of the Jews?" Jesus answered, "Do you ask this on your own, or did others tell you about me?" Pilate replied, "I am not a Jew, am I? Your own nation and the chief priests have handed you over to me. What have you done?" Jesus answered, "My kingdom is not from this world. If my kingdom were from this world, my followers would be fighting to keep me from being handed over to the Jews. But, as it is, my kingdom is not from here." Pilate asked him, "So you are a king?" Jesus answered, "You say that I

*am a king. For this I was born, and for this I came
into the world, to testify to the truth. Everyone who
belongs to the truth listens to my voice." Pilate
asked him, "What is truth?"* (John 18: 33-38)

A Personal Journey:

As the summer holidays wind down, a column about
"work" may not be the most welcome piece of
literature you're going to read this week. But, here it
is!

Please bear with me. There's a point I'd like to
make. The point is that there is an enormous chasm
in our lives between what passes for work and what
passes for play. Often we don't just look forward to
our holidays as a nice change of pace, we literally live
for them. We're desperate for them.

Money and a decent holiday, for many of us, are the
only real reasons to work. Which means, basically,
that we are content to spend our lives offering a
pound of flesh for an ounce of satisfaction.

Work is a means to an end. It occupies our lives but
it's disconnected from who we are. Work is what we
do, but "all the rest," including holidays, is who we
really are.

Consider, for a moment, the working day. For many
people, it means starting out with family. We try to
connect with family members about what their days
are going to be like. We encourage them. We find ways
to support them and meet their needs. We do all that
we can to exercise a genuine set of family values.

Then, we go off to work. All of a sudden, we're
putting on our "game face."

All the supportive values that are important to us in
real life fly out the window of our new Buick like an
old candy wrapper.

This is business! It's a dog-eat-dog world of winners
and losers. No excuses. Get it done well and get it

done consistently. What's going on in your life takes a back seat to what you can produce. If Jones slips up then Jones is gone, and you may get his job.

At the end of the day, we come home again and morph back into the kind and caring person we are in "real life."

Michael Stephen, past chairman of Aetna International, is an author and a popular speaker at business seminars and conferences. He debunks the Dr. Jekyll and Mr. Hyde approach our society takes in dividing our "work" lives from our "real" lives.

At a recent seminar in Waterloo, Ontario, Stephen said that we should never leave our values at the door when it comes to our work. Maintaining our values and our total spirituality is key to creating a positive, caring, thriving, and productive workplace.

Far from burying our values, Stephen wants us to celebrate them and exercise them at work just as we do at home. There should be no disconnect between our work values and our real values if the workplace is to become a positive part of our lives.

Smart businesses, Stephen said, care about what's in the hearts and minds of their employees. That's the "competitive advantage" in today's world.

Stephen, author of *Spirituality in Business: The Hidden Success Factor*, believes a dearth of human spirituality, a disconnect with our value systems, led to the greed, dishonesty, and arrogance that brought down such business giants as Enron and WorldCom.

There should never be a disconnect, he says, between what you do for work and how you live— between the business world and the "real" world. People who genuinely understand that half the world works for less than two dollars a day, he adds, aren't inclined to be wasteful and dishonest with money. What we value should be who we are, whether we're at work or at home. The spirit should be alive in us at all times.

Holidays, of course, are wonderful things. They rejuvenate us. They offer us refreshment and new perspectives. Most importantly, they're something different and they're fun.

The message of Michael Stephen is that we need to create a world in which the joy of holidays is rivaled by the genuine spiritual satisfaction of our work.

A Time for Reflection:

Make a list of the top 10 things you consider to be your key values (e.g. honesty, kindness, tolerance, diligence, loyalty, forgiveness, etc.). Are these values firm for you in every situation or are they flexible and situational? What kind of value do you place on your values? Are you happy with the way you live out your values? What would you change?

In the scripture, do you think Jesus and Pilate are really connecting or communicating with one another? What is it about their respective value systems that places them so far apart in the world? What does Pilate mean when he asks, "What is truth?"

In your working world (whether volunteer or paid) do you feel a genuine disconnect between your real values and your "business" activities? Name some examples. Why does this disconnect exist? Who causes it?

Why is caring about what's in the hearts and minds of employees considered (by some) a "competitive advantage" in today's business world?

What we value should be who we are, whether we're at work or at home. What would happen in your "working" world if you were to live this statement out in an open and honest way? How would it impact your work relationships? Would it change your own feelings towards your workplace? What would it take to honour your spirituality in the workplace?

A Time for Prayer:

Gracious God, help us to find integrity in our lives. Help us to honour Jesus Christ our Lord by consistently living the values he has shown us, in all the situations that we face day in and day out. Help us to know in our hearts that whether we're with family and friends or whether we're in our places of "business" we belong to Christ. In all the challenging and complex situations we encounter guide us to respond from the grace and power of Christ within us. Guide us, God, to be true to our values and to be honest and honourable servants of your kingdom. Amen.

A Time for Action:

Centre yourself as one who belongs to Christ. Make a promise to yourself, before God, that "what you value is who you are" and that you will carry your values consistently whether you're at home or at work. Define what that means in the challenges you currently face, and act accordingly.

Dean Salter

Week 36: Imagine What Can Happen Here

In the second creation story of Genesis, God puts the first human in the garden to care for it and benefit from it. The garden belongs to God and life in such a rich and bountiful setting is a gift to be treasured and respected. The only stricture is to stay clear of "the tree of the knowledge of good and evil." In other words, life is about obeying God and living in harmony. It's not about control; it's not about trying to *be* God. To play God is to court death and destruction.

The Lord God took the man and put him in the garden of Eden to till and keep it. And the Lord God commanded man, "You may freely eat of every tree of the garden; but of the tree of the knowledge of good and evil you shall not eat, for in the day that you eat of it you shall die." (Genesis 2: 15-17)

A Personal Journey:
As I was driving home from Toronto the other day a real estate sign planted in the middle of a farm field caught my eye. The billboard-style "for sale" sign, hovering over a ripening field of wheat, read, "Imagine What Can Happen Here!"

The very creative, eye-catching advertisement implies, of course, that this fertile field will one day be turned into housing or perhaps another high-powered commercial development of the sort that already crowds the western borders of Toronto.

"Imagine what can happen here!" I found the phrase both disturbing and challenging. There is a very deep part of my faith that calls me to be a good "gardener" on this planet, showing all the love and care I can muster for God's created world. The sign disturbed me because it served to remind me of my limitations as a faithful gardener. I live in a good-sized house that's perched, along with a hundred other houses, on some of the best farmland in Ontario. I followed a certain baby boomer imperative that placed many of us in single family homes "with property," near the big cities. Somewhere along the line I've confused gardening with subdividing and bulldozing. Mea culpa!

"Imagine what can happen here!" Let's look at what's already happened to the "garden." Today, close to one-half of all Canada's urbanized land is built right on top of our best agricultural land. Over the past 50 years the supply of dependable agricultural land across Canada has declined by 4 percent over against a steadily growing population that now exceeds 30 million people. Fifty years ago 38 percent of Canada's population was rural. Today, only 16 percent of Canadians live in rural areas. The bulk of the evidence suggests that we're not gardening God's good earth so much as we're paving it!

It's easy to sit back and broadly lay blame for Canada's diminishing farmland; for our diminishing ability to feed ourselves. We can blame the farmer for wanting to sell his or her land. But produce and livestock prices are often so low that farming is a tough, hand-to-mouth business that's hard on individuals and hard on families. Why wouldn't you sell the farm for big money if you could? We can blame the realtors and developers. But they're just doing their work—meeting an economic demand. We can blame ourselves for creating that demand. But, while we can change the shape of the demand, the demand itself isn't likely to go away. We can blame the government, of course. But governments aren't as laissez-faire as we sometimes think in releasing farmland for development. Regulations to protect farmland do exist. It's not as if our leaders have never heard about this issue. We could blame history. After all, most of our major Canadian settlements were intentionally built near good farmland because agriculture was central to their economies and their survival. But blaming history is tantamount to throwing our hands hopelessly in the air and saying that the die is cast and there's nothing we can do about our diminishing ability to feed ourselves and provide food support to the needy worldwide.

"Imagine what can happen here!" The challenge we face is not to point a finger at anyone for our diminishing farmlands. Heaping blame is an easy "out." The challenge is for all of us to take responsibility; to recognize that this is a very complex issue that requires creative "imaginings" from all of us.

For example, I can imagine an economic system that pays the farmer a fair price for his or her produce or livestock; a system that makes keeping the farm far more attractive than selling it for development. I can imagine even more stringent regulations on the development of our dependable agricultural land, with stronger incentives to build on less arable land. I can imagine more encouragement to build up, using less land, rather than building out in sprawling developments. I can imagine governments across Canada establishing more untouchable agricultural reserves to protect the best farmland in the country. I can imagine trying to become a better gardener in God's world by learning two things: what it actually means to be a gardener and what it actually means to live in God's world.

I'm not the greatest "imaginer" in the world. I think you can all do better than my "for examples." Please do so and share your ideas with your community leaders. Communities together have a great capacity (sometimes untapped) for looking at the land around us and imagining what needs to happen there in order for us to live well and keep the "garden" healthy.

A Time for Reflection:

If we don't "own" or "control" creation, what is our place in the natural world? Who are we called to be in God's world?

The air is toxic, the waters are polluted, and the ground is either exhausted or paved over. Why have we failed the garden so badly? Where do you see hope for the future?

In the "Personal Journey" above it's claimed that we can "change the shape" of our own demands in order to preserve valuable farmland. What have your traditional "demands" been and how would you re-shape them?

In your mind's eye, place yourself in a farm field on the outskirts of a big city. What are the best things you can imagine happening on this field to honour God's creation? What are the worst things you can imagine? Try making a list of possibilities.

What practical steps can you imagine that would help your community preserve its best farmland?

A Time for Prayer:

Gracious God, we confess that we've taken the gift of being allowed to live with respect in creation and covered it with layer upon layer of our own toxic greed. In our drive for more and more wealth we've destroyed species, polluted the air, water, and earth, and paved the land that feeds us. We have tried to play God and each day we push our planet closer and closer to death. Loving God, teach us how to garden. Open our hearts, finally, to understand our place in creation; our place in your world. Hear our prayer. Amen.

A Time for Action:

Either individually or as part of a group, define what you are willing to do in order to protect your community's best farmland. List your firmest, most committed "to do's" and brainstorm an action plan for each one. Take your first "to do" and make it happen.

Week 37: Measure for Measure

Too often, it feels like our entire western culture is based on the premise that there are "good guys" and "bad guys" in this world. The "good guys" (that's us) are justified in using whatever nasty little devices we can dream up in order to preserve our way of life from the "bad guys"(that's them). In fact, the popular culture these days celebrates violence as never before—and extreme, unfettered violence "to preserve our freedoms" is considered the height of bravery and patriotism. We no longer treasure justice and reason as the core of our democracy. We place our money on being more violent than those "outsiders" who seek to terrorize us and bend us to their will. We seek to beat them at their own "game" without the slightest understanding of who they are and what their game might be.

Can anyone define what our way of life is? Is it possible we've already given it away; surrendered its strength and virtue through the white flag of ignorance and paranoia?

"Do not judge, and you will not be judged; do not condemn, and you will not be condemned. Forgive, and you will be forgiven; give, and it will be given to you. A good measure, pressed down, shaken together, running over, will be put in your lap; for the measure you give will be the measure you get back." (Luke 6: 37-38)

A Personal Journey:

It's hard to live on this planet today and not have some personal thoughts about the events of September 11, 2001.

As we approach another anniversary of 9/11, we'll once again be vividly reminded of the horrific attack on the twin towers of the World Trade Center in New York that killed thousands of innocent people. We'll remember Pennsylvania and the Pentagon. We'll mourn the victims of 9/11 once again in sadness and respect.

Once again, we'll be reminded of the heroism of the rescuers. We'll have the relatively brief history of the War on Terrorism recounted and analyzed repeatedly. It certainly gives no joy to reflect on 9/11, but it feels necessary because our world has changed so much since then and is in danger of changing much more.

My own thoughts on 9/11 have no more currency than anyone else's. They're personal thoughts and I share them because I can. My personal thoughts are shaped by the fact I'm a Christian, although many other Christians may see things differently.

As we approach the anniversary of 9/11, the first thing that occurs to me is how completely understandable the global response was in the early days and months. An unspeakable act of evil was perpetrated that cost thousands of innocent lives. The global community, across all religious faiths and most nations, called for justice, without specifying exactly what that would mean.

The tragedy of 9/11, of course, led directly to the ongoing, seemingly endless war in Afghanistan. But, to this day, there is general confusion in the body politic about what would finally constitute justice for the victims of 9/11.

Still lost in the rhetoric of war is any real understanding of the "other side." Why is there such palpable hatred of "The West" in some quarters?

While not condoning terrorists or terrorism, is it possible to believe that their support springs from people who feel a stinging sense of injustice and degradation which they blame on "The West?" What would it mean to truly address that sense of injustice?

The second thing that occurs to me is what a dangerous crossroads we're standing at right now. There's a scripture passage that I find very powerful. It says very simply, "Do not judge, and you will not be judged; do not condemn, and you will not be condemned."

In a blind and foolish act of retribution against a leader they disliked, our greatest ally and friend, the United States, judged and condemned Iraq and launched a naked war of aggression against them, tying it by a tenuous thread to the War on Terrorism.

How many nations could be bombed into cinders (Iran, Syria, North Korea, Cuba, Venezuela, etc., etc.) because the world's only superpower decides they're unacceptable? What would it say about us as Canadians and what we're becoming if we support a foreign policy of pre-emptive violence? What happens in the national psyche when we develop a predilection for judging, condemning, and attacking rather than searching for common ground and resolution? What happens when we substitute blind judgment for humanity; when we substitute condemnation for authentic moral fibre?

I think if that day comes then terrorism will have succeeded. It will have forced us to deny our principles and become the very thing we despise—the very thing most terrorist supporters believe we already are.

To reflect on the horrors of 9/11 is cause to shudder—not just for the past, but for the future as well.

A Time for Reflection:

As Canadians, what would you say "our way of life" actually is? What values do we hold in common as Canadians?

Take a moment to reflect on this week's scripture passage. What do you think would happen if you lived this passage out in day to day life? What would happen if Canada accepted those concepts as the basis for its foreign policy?

What do you think would happen in conflict situations if we tried to understand "the other side"—tried to discover the roots of their anger? Where would it lead us? Why is this discipline hard for both people and nations?

Why has violence become so prevalent in everything from the games we play to the conduct of our foreign policy worldwide? What is the hold that violence has on us?

How would we know, here in Canada, if terrorism was victorious? What would be different; what would stay the same?

A Time for Prayer:

Gracious God, make me a channel of your peace: where there is hatred, let me bring your love; where there is injury, your healing power, and where there's doubt, true faith in you. Make me a channel of your peace: where there is despair in life, let me bring hope, where there is darkness, only light; and where there's sadness, ever joy. Make me a channel of your peace: It is in pardoning that we are pardoned, in giving to all that we receive, and in dying that we're born to eternal life. Spirit, grant that I may never seek so much to be consoled as to console, to be understood as to understand, to be loved as to love with all my soul. Amen. (based on the words of St. Francis Assisi, circa 1220)

A Time for Action:

Take more time, and make a greater effort, to learn about "the other side" in situations of conflict, whether they be personal or global. Without judgment or condemnation, discover what drives the other side; discover the source of their anger. The measure you give will be the measure you get. Decide what measure you are able to give and offer it as a gift to God.

Week 38: Giving Back

There's little question we live in an era that worships "celebrity." Countless photos, voluminous amounts of text, and ubiquitous television programs have no other purpose than to capture the "news" about our favourite stars. Many of these stars seem to exist less on talent than on notoriety, designer clothing, and someone else's money. With notable exceptions, they are ponderously, voraciously self-involved.

These time-dated celebrities have creative ways of grabbing attention. But, are they successful people? Perhaps the kindest thing we can say is "not yet." Truly successful people have learned that they're not the centre of the universe. They've learned that they're part of a wider community. Whatever success they've had in life, they owe a strong measure of thanks to family, friends, teachers, and mentors along the way. Successful people know that the greatest measure of their success isn't what they *have* but, rather, what they're willing to *give* back to their community.

Who is wise and understanding among you? Show by your good life that your works are done with gentleness born of wisdom. But if you have bitter envy and selfish ambition in your hearts, do not be boastful and false to the truth. Such wisdom does not come from above, but is earthly, unspiritual, devilish. For where there is envy and selfish ambition, there will also be disorder and wickedness of every kind. But the wisdom from above is first pure, then peaceable, gentle, willing to yield, full of mercy and good fruits, without a trace of partiality or hypocrisy. And a harvest of righteousness is sown in peace for those who make peace. (James 3: 13-18)

A Personal Journey:

Several years ago, before his death from cancer, I read an article about famous talk show host Johnny Carson that really impressed me.

The 2003 article said that Mr. Carson, in the 11 years since his retirement from the Tonight Show, had been donating substantial sums of money in support of various groups and causes in his old hometown of Norfolk, Nebraska. Five million dollars to that point. His generosity had helped to fund a cancer centre, a high school theatre, a public library, an arts centre, a museum, and a research and learning centre.

One could be cynical about this, of course. You might say, "OK, so what's the big deal? A multi-millionaire donated a few million dollars over time to his little home town. So what! It's not like he couldn't afford it. And, it's a sweet tax write-off anyway." But one could also decide not to be cynical. Here was a man who didn't have to donate a dime to anyone. But, he quietly donated millions to his old hometown as a way of honouring the strength and values of his rural upbringing—as a way of helping to maintain those values for others.

In the article, Mr. Carson described growing up in Norfolk as "an era that gave you a direction in your life."

As I read the article I remember feeling a great deal of respect for Mr. Carson. He honoured his roots and tried to encourage the spirit and values that gave him a good start in life. But, what really impressed me is that the one-time "King of Late Night" offered a fundamental mission statement that was clearly the foundation for his generosity.

Mr. Carson said, "If anyone is lucky enough to accumulate enough funds to live better than you have a right to, then you have a moral obligation to give something back."

Those are critically important words because they define how we see ourselves and our "neighbours" in this world. Mr. Carson was saying, I think, that "a successful person" is built by the love, support, and mentoring of others. The successful person's fire and determination are supported and encouraged along the way, and even such words as "luck" and "opportunity" have had human faces for these individuals.

It's also true, Mr. Carson might have added, that the world is full of "neighbours" who have had no such good fortune in their lives. They've received no love, support, or mentoring. They were never encouraged and they never had a good opportunity open up for them. Their lives have been a long, hard struggle. "Successful" people understand the nature of gift and opportunity. They understand how easy it is for people to be pushed to the margins of society and written off.

"Successful" people are those who will not give up on their neighbours. They know how tenuous life is and how fortunate they themselves have been to receive gifts and opportunities. They cherish those gifts and opportunities for others.

As Mr. Carson said, "...you have a moral obligation to give something back."

A Time for Reflection:
What do you think is the difference between celebrity and success? Can you name celebrities who are also successful people? In what ways do you feel "successful" yourself?

Reflect on this week's scripture passage, particularly on "the wisdom from above." How does this wisdom relate to the "success" of human beings?

Did you have "an era that gave you a direction in your life?" Who were your mentors and role models? When and how did you decide on the direction for your life? Who builds "successful" people, in your opinion?

Who builds unsuccessful people? What are the influences that tear people down?

Why do successful people care about those who are in need? Why is there "a moral obligation to give something back" to our community?

A Time for Prayer:

Gracious God, help us to receive with open hearts the wisdom from above. May we celebrate all that is pure, gentle, willing to yield, and full of mercy and good fruits. May we live with our neighbours without partiality or hypocrisy. May we live as those who honour all the gracious gifts we've received from our community and may we always have the generosity of spirit to give back more than we've received. May we always understand that what we have and what we give is from the bounty of Christ our Lord. Amen.

A Time for Action:

You are a successful person. You have a moral obligation to give something back to the community as a person who has learned what it means to *be* a "neighbour" and to *have* a "neighbour." Spend some time in prayer. Decide what your gift will be, then give it.

Week 39: The Soul of Generosity

Last week we focused on the fact successful people know how much they've been given by the "community" and feel a moral obligation to "give back." They want others to have the same opportunities they've had to live successful lives. Successful people understand what it means to *be* a neighbour and to *have* a neighbour both locally and globally. But, understanding a moral obligation and being intrinsically generous are two different things. Do you find generosity an easy concept? In each situation of life do you immediately grasp what's the truly "generous" thing to do? And are you thrilled to do it? For many of us, generosity is a bit of a murky subject, sandwiched somewhere between the call to be "good" and the concern for being duped. For many of us it's just not as easy as it looks.

The point is this: the one who sows sparingly will also reap sparingly, and the one who sows bountifully will also reap bountifully. Each of you must give as you have made up your mind, not reluctantly or under compulsion, for God loves a cheerful giver.
(2 Corinthians 9: 6-7)

A Personal Journey:
Some years ago, I traveled to Edmonton for a weekend meeting on a topic that seemed important at

the time. I can't remember what it was exactly, or who was there, or what was decided, but I strongly recollect the urgency of the gathering. The mind does play tricks because the only thing I remember clearly is Sunday morning. A group of us decided to attend worship at a fledgling little church, just before heading to the airport for our flights home.

The service proceeded in the usual way, pushing inexorably towards the offering, when it dawned on me that the only money I had in my possession was a $20 bill. I had guarded the twenty over the weekend so I'd have enough money for a taxi to the airport. Now the offering plate was making its way closer to me. Should I follow the minister's advice and give generously, swearing off all selfish thoughts, or should I hang onto that twenty for dear life?

Suffice to say that I didn't miss my flight. I brought the bill out of my pocket, stared at it like a cut diamond, and stuffed it back in with a furtive glance to the right and left.

After the service, the man next to me, who happened to be an adult education teacher, turned to me and said, "You might like to take my course on generosity." And, of course, he said it without a hint of malice or harshness—just a quiet whisper of pity for a fallen brother. "Yes," I said, looking for an escape route. "That's probably a good idea."

This little story came to mind the other day when a friend told me about a close encounter with generosity that he'd experienced at a local Tim Horton's. He was in the drive-through and when he pulled up to the window to pay the usual $1.39 for a large double-double he was told that the previous customer had covered the price of his coffee.

This, of course, was a generous act—and certainly not the first time this has happened in our community. But, you see, it raised that niggling question of whether my own sense of generosity would ever allow me to carry out such an unselfish act. What if one day I should boldly resolve, no matter what, to pay the freight for the car behind me in the Tim's lineup? It would be just my luck that he was the new guy in the office, charged with buying lunch for the whole gang at accounts receivable. "You said what? His bill is $89???!!!"

To tell you the truth, this whole generosity thing seems fraught with difficulties and dangers. It seems downright unnatural, when you're brought up to know the value of a dollar and the boundless joy of acquisition, to turn around and actually give something away.

I've heard people say that we're all "naturally" generous. But, I'm not so sure. I think my church "friend" in Edmonton was onto something. Maybe generosity needs to be studied, thought about, argued about, and improved like a too-rusty golf swing. Maybe we can't just take it for granted. Maybe we can't just assume we'll know what it is when the time comes. It could be that the last thing a skid road wino needs is a quarter out of your pocket. Or maybe your teenager doesn't really need the extra $20.

I'm pretty sure I could use a good six-week course on the true nature of generosity. I don't need much guidance in "acquiring" and "protecting" but I would sure like to find a clear window to the other side. In this world, I think generosity isn't some gentle little loose end that will take care of itself. It requires the same hard-nosed dedication we've always reserved for acquiring all the "things" we want. None of us glides effortlessly into generosity. It's vital, but it's by no means "natural."

A Time for Reflection:
Do you find that "being generous" comes easily to you? Do you think of yourself as a naturally generous

person? How would you define the concept of generosity in your own mind? What kind of boundaries do you place on it?

"God loves a cheerful giver." What are the qualities of a cheerful giver? Why would it be of any importance to God whether the giver is cheerful or not?

If you only had $20 to your name to pay for a taxi to the airport would you drop it in the Sunday morning offering plate anyway? What would such an action say about your sense of "generosity?"

How do you know if what you're doing is generosity or foolishness? Does the begging wino need a quarter from you? Does your teenager need an extra $20?

"The one who sows sparingly will reap sparingly." How does this Bible verse impact your understanding of generosity?

If you were to take a course on generosity, what are the top five questions you'd like to ask the class?

A Time for Prayer:

Gracious God, help us to understand what is true, just, and loving as we try to live healthy, faithful lives in this world. Grant us an understanding of what generosity really looks like through the powerful filter of your Kingdom. Grant us the courage to act generously in a world which is not generous and to give cheerfully in a world which better understands greed than gift. Amen.

A Time for Action:

Think of a gift that you've wanted to give for some time. It could be a "thing" or it could be an action that you've wanted to "gift" to another. Is it a good and faithful gift? If so, clearly define what stands in the way of your giving it. Weigh your concerns against "Kingdom love" and "Kingdom generosity." Make your decision and act accordingly.

Week 40: No Time for Stereotypes

Keep an open mind. It's one of those phrases that gets repeated over and over by liberal-minded folk wherever you find them.

Keep an open mind. It should be a no-brainer. Of course we should keep an open mind. What right do we have to come to quick judgment about the people and events which surround us? "Judge not, lest ye be judged." There's always a story beneath the story and we should give people the benefit of the doubt.

This all sounds good on paper but, in the real world, how many of us can *keep an open mind* when it comes to things that matter to us? From the price of gas to our daughter's latest boyfriend, we make snap judgments that are quite often based more on heat than light. Perhaps, the first question we should ask ourselves is, 'What does an open mind actually look like?' Is it an empty mind? Is it a mind incapable of making judgments? Or is it something else?

As Jesus was walking along, he saw a man called Matthew sitting at the tax booth; and he said to him, "Follow me." And he got up and followed him.

And as he sat at dinner in the house, many tax collectors and sinners came and were sitting with him and his disciples. When the Pharisees saw this, they said to his disciples, "Why does your teacher eat with tax collectors and sinners?" But, when he heard this, he said, "Those who are well have no need of a physician, but those who are sick. Go and learn what this means, 'I desire mercy, not sacrifice.' For I have come to call not the righteous but sinners." (Matthew 9: 9-13)

A Personal Journey:

It was the spring of 1986 and I was on a working visit to several African countries. My colleagues told me to expect problems at the borders. Many customs agents, they said, were corrupt and expected bribes in order to pass "wealthy" westerners into their countries. So when I came upon my first customs agent in Kenya I was prepared for a rough ride. I fingered the bills in my pocket, wondering when the right time would be to buy my way into the country. The agent gave me a quick look, checked through my luggage with a scowl on his face, and then looked me straight in the eye. This, I thought, must be the moment. But, just as I was about to pull the money out, the agent smiled broadly and said, "Jambo. You may proceed."

I felt like an idiot, of course. I'd bought hook, line, and sinker into a stereotype. I assumed that because this was an African customs agent then he must be poor and he must be "on the take."

It's easy to sink into stereotyping people. Don has no ambition; Karen can't make a decision; Bill won't stand up for himself. It's a way of ordering and pigeon-holing people to our own advantage. If we box them up in just the right way we can control them—limit their potential to challenge, upset, or surprise us.

One of the groups we love to stereotype is the oil companies. They're the demon seed of our society, out to make outrageous profits with little concern for gas prices paid by "the little guy" and no concern whatsoever for the environment.

As a liberal Christian, it's practically a right of passage for me to feel some animosity towards "big oil." But, how much is truth and how much is stereotype? I was surprised the other day to see an article in the newspaper quoting Jeroen Van Der Veer, Chief Executive Officer of Royal Dutch Shell, on global warming. "For us as a company," he said, "the debate over CO_2 is over. We've entered a debate about what we can do about it." He added that energy companies would be ready to work with governments to solve the carbon problem if there was a worldwide framework to bind governments to the same standards. The Kyoto Accord, which binds 35 countries to curb greenhouse gases, was a good start, he said. Pushing the discussion further, he challenged the United States, which produces 25 percent of all greenhouse gases, to embrace Kyoto. "Why don't you (the U.S.) join the Kyoto agreement?" Van Der Veer asked an American participant at a meeting of political and business leaders in Dubai. "You see an initial framework there and you can build on that for our future." He noted that Shell is currently looking for ways to cut CO_2 emissions by trapping the gas created in their production processes and then injecting it underground into their oilfields to increase pressure and enhance the recovery of oil.

Before reading that article I'd always assumed that oil companies were totally oblivious to global warming and solidly lined up against the Kyoto Accord. Now, here's the head of Royal Dutch Shell plumping for Kyoto and willing to be part of a global solution to what he acknowledges as a serious problem. If my stereotype of big oil isn't entirely shattered it's at least seriously dented. Maybe it's time to keep an open mind?

Jesus had no time for stereotypes. If he'd cared about stereotypes why would he have chosen Matthew, the tax collector, as one of his 12 disciples? Few in Israel were despised and mistrusted as much as those who collected taxes for the Roman occupiers. And yet, Matthew was among the chosen few who were trusted to learn the gospel and spread it. If Jesus worried about stereotypes, why would he have held up the importance of women in ministry and in society? Jesus never accepted the stereotypical role of women in his society as little more than possessions. In his eyes, both men and women were equally loved and gifted by God.

Like Jesus, people of faith should have no room for stereotypes. Whether they're customs agents, oil company leaders, co-workers, friends, or family, people shouldn't be put into stagnant, lifeless boxes that we label and set aside. People should be honoured for their potential and celebrated for their fruits. Through Christ we know we can never be allowed to use stereotypes to rob people of their humanity.

A Time for Reflection:

What does an open mind actually look like? How do you know if you're keeping an open mind? Can you name situations where keeping an open mind has proven difficult? Why is it difficult?

Reread this week's scripture passage. What is the point Jesus is trying to make to Matthew in asking him to be a disciple? What is the point he's trying to make to the Pharisees about the Kingdom of God?

Does it surprise you that the CEO of Royal Dutch Shell recognizes the problem of global warming and supports the Kyoto Accord? What's your own "gut reaction" to big oil in the world today? Do they want to fight global warming? Will they cooperate? What's their bottom line? Where do your stereotypes come into play?

What role should governments play in the struggle against global warming? Which governments are taking the lead? Which are not? Where do your stereotypes come into play?

The values of the Kingdom of God should be brought to bear against the values which underlie global warming and climate change. How do these values differ? Who's the good guy? Who's the bad guy? How do stereotypes stand in the way of cooperative action and problem solving?

A Time for Prayer:

Gracious God, help us to be a force for unity in this world. Give us the strength and wisdom to live a discipleship which draws people together to heal wounds and find common solutions to our problems. Help us to hear the truths of others and joyfully share our own truths. May we, in Christ's name, give up the search for adversaries and open our hearts to neighbours instead. Through your grace, we can be a community with an open mind and an open hand. Amen.

A Time for Action:

Learn everything you can about global warming and climate change. The DVD of "An Inconvenient Truth" is a good starting point. Educate others. Eliminate all stereotypes. Do not search for bad guys and good guys, only for partners who are willing to solve the problem. Form a study/action group in your church. Take the personal steps in your own home or office that help combat global warming, and encourage others to do the same. By petitions, letters, and phone calls, urge governments and companies to work as partners in supporting and meeting the commitments of the Kyoto Accord.

Dean Salter

Week 41: Be Thankful That News is News

The world is going to hell in a hand basket. It's easy to reach that conclusion when you listen to the television news or read your daily newspaper. Acts of violence seem commonplace, oppression is rife, the environment is under siege, and countless nations seem to be at war or on the brink of war. Have things become so bad "out there" that all we can do is keep our heads down and "look after our own?" Has our world become so corrupt and damaged that we have little choice but to write it off? And, what would happen if we did?

The Lord is my shepherd, I shall not want. He makes me lie down in green pastures; he leads me beside still waters; he restores my soul. He leads me in right paths for his name's sake. Even though I walk through the darkest valley, I fear no evil; for you are with me; your rod and your staff—they comfort me. You prepare a table before me in the presence of my enemies; you anoint my head with oil; my cup overflows. Surely goodness and mercy shall follow me all the days of my life, and I shall dwell in the house of the Lord my whole life long. (Psalm 23)

A Personal Journey:

I was studying the front section of the newspaper the other day and, quite frankly, I felt a little depressed.

225

Being a fan of the daily paper, I usually read voraciously through every section and feel all the better for being informed of the day's news and events. But, last week, after reading the front section and reflecting on all the stories together, I got the depressing feeling that the world was becoming unglued.

In the span of a few pages I read that U.S. President George W. Bush is getting more and more anxious to go to war with Iraq, that Osama Bin Laden is planning more attacks on the West, and that a sniper in the Washington, D.C. area may be targeting children. On top of that, Ontario may be facing an energy shortage next summer, special needs children may not be getting the help they need, Israeli raids are continuing against Palestinian militants, a fuel tanker had exploded in Yemen, religious repression exists in many countries throughout the world, and AIDS is contributing to a growing famine across southern Africa. *(This column was written in 2002 but you'll notice that our "news" hasn't changed that much — - D.S.)*

I don't know why, all of a sudden, the same news stories that kept me "in touch" and "informed" one day would depress me the next. In retrospect, it probably has to do with losing some perspective on how the world really is. It's not that hard to fall into an anxious funk when the world is pictured, day in and day out, in newspapers and magazines, on radio, television, and the Internet, as being a troubled place. When you see the downside in such volume, it's easy to picture the world as coming unglued.

A wise newsperson once said to me, "They don't call it 'news' for nothing. It's our job to let people know what's happened in the world today that's really new, that's out of the ordinary, unusual, odd, and abnormal. If the dog bites the mail carrier, we don't report it. If the mail carrier bites the dog, it's going to be front page. It's unusual, it's different, it doesn't happen every day."

Maybe the very thing that makes "Thanksgiving" possible in our world it the fact the mail carrier very seldom bites the dog. The front section of the newspaper has some critical information for us to know about the world. But, the fact is, the front section doesn't tell us about the whole world—only a tiny fraction of it.

It doesn't tell us about what our lives are like day to day. It doesn't tell us about homes and families, work and play. It doesn't tell us about friends, about beautiful places, and about the small things that are accomplished each day. It doesn't tell us about systems that work or people who demonstrate their love in quiet ways. It doesn't discuss the subtle things that inspire us and give us life and hope in the world.

So, the bottom line here is that if I'm slipping into an anxious funk over the front section of my newspaper, I need to get over it. I want the news, I care about the news, and I feel like I need the news to be a good citizen of my community and my world. But, I also need to give thanks for the vast majority of the world which will never find its way into the front section.

That's also the world I live in. It's the world I celebrate and it's the world that informs my daily life. There's a great deal to be thankful for in that world.

A Time for Reflection:

Name five things about the "front page" world that really concern you. Do you think these five situations are hopeless and impossible to resolve?

Name five things in your life that give you energy and hope.

How do you weigh the relative importance of all ten things in your life? Does your response have an impact on how you respond to the "situations" named above?

Discuss what constitutes "news" in our world. Why are the stories chosen? What is the best possible perspective we can bring to living with "the news?"

The 23rd Psalm was chosen as this week's scripture reading. Re-read the Psalm very slowly and deliberately. What perspective does it give you on God's world and God's care for you in an imperfect world? If the shepherd "restores your soul," what does that mean for your actions in the world?

Many people find it difficult to offer "thanksgiving" for what they see as a hopelessly broken world. As a person of faith, what is at the "heart" of your thanksgiving?

A Time for Prayer:

Loving God, you walk with me through the darkest valleys of my life—past, present, and future. You are the green pastures; you are the still waters of my life. You are comfort, mercy, love, and perseverance for me. In the face of a thousand broken vessels scattered over the earth, you show me millions which are able to hold the waters of life and I feel hope. But, you do not want me to dwell on the millions. In the power of hope you challenge me, as your servant, to pray for the broken vessels of the world and to walk as a healer among them. Gracious God, you are the centre of life, the source of all abundance, and the heart of all purpose. To you I give thanksgiving every day. Amen.

A Time for Action:

What would it take for you to be the one person in your club, committee, family, or other grouping who does not believe "the world is going to hell in a hand basket?" Can you be the person who offers hope (through words and/or deeds) when those around you are falling into cynicism and despair? Find that very important person inside of yourself.

Week 42: Starry, Starry Night

Since we have to live with ourselves more or less constantly from cradle to grave, it's hard not to exaggerate our own importance. Our failures are so epic and devastating that they must surely send shockwaves down the halls of humanity. Our successes are so brilliant and seminal that the forward march of all creation must surely be evident. Encased in our own daily dramas, it's hard to imagine that we're anything but the centre of our own reality. It's hard to imagine that, beyond our own successes and failures, anything matters very much. And then, if we're lucky, God will show us a starry, starry night.

Happy are those who find wisdom, and those who get understanding, for her income is better than silver, and her revenue better than gold. She is more precious than jewels, and nothing you desire can compare with her. Long life is in her right hand; in her left hand are riches and honor. Her ways are ways of pleasantness, and all her paths are peace. She is a tree of life to those who lay hold of her; those who hold her fast are called happy. (Proverbs 3: 13-18)

A Personal Journey:
A few weeks ago, the lights went out in north Waterloo. Apparently, a squirrel, for reasons we'll never totally understand, hurled itself into a

transformer and shorted out the electricity to hundreds of residences—including my own. Since there was also no power at my mother-in-law's apartment five minutes down the road, I naturally assumed that all of North America had been, once again, plunged into darkness. For nearly an hour I searched stations on my transistor radio for information on this disaster. Nothing. Just music and happy talk. How insidious is that! Terrorists everywhere!

Then, just as the lights came on, I caught a local newscast that described the problem, detailing the squirrel's horrible fate. The world itself seemed intact—at least for the moment.

I may have over-reacted a bit. After all, power outages haven't been uncommon on our little grid over the past year. But, it's hard not to think about the Great Blackout of August 2003 every time the lights go out. Millions of people in northeastern North America were without power for long hours, even days. Livelihoods were damaged and lives were put at risk. Without question, those were tough and dangerous times for many people. There was no terrorism involved, of course, but many did raise the alarm, as they always do when something unusual happens.

For me, the Great Blackout was more inconvenient than dangerous. There was no television to occupy my time and it was also pretty challenging for my wife and I to put a meal together. But, believe it or not, my overwhelming memory of the blackout is that it was an "opportunity." I've never been one to see a silver lining in every cloud. I don't believe every problem has a wonderful lesson to share. Some problems are just painful, day in and day out, and we struggle to live through them with as much courage as we can muster.

But, some problems are "opportunities" and, for me, the blackout was a case in point. When it was clear that the blackout was going to last for a long time, my wife and I spread an old blanket on the front lawn and we spent the evening staring at the stars. Of course, without city lights the stars are brilliant.

When the world goes quiet; when all the artificial power we generate is shut down; when we stare up at the cosmos literally white with stars, there's an opportunity to reflect—something we don't do very often. In the firestorm of everyday living, for better or worse, we often become the epicentre of our own little universes. But, when the artificial power is shut down and the stars take over the sky, there can be this realization that we're a tiny part of a greater whole. We've been given a tiny place in the miracle of the universe. We've been given the gift of community—a tiny speck in a sea of communities.

As I lay there on the blanket, I didn't feel tiny, hopeless, and lost. That wasn't the "message" at all. The message was an awesome verification that, in spite of my behaviour sometimes, I'm just not the centre of the universe.

The metaphor of the stars gives us an opportunity to "re-imagine" our lives. What does it mean when artificial power stops shielding the universe? How do we act in community when we stop seeing ourselves as the centre of our own little universes; when we begin to see ourselves as a small part of a greater whole? If life is a gift, what does it mean to be a gifted part of that great universe of stars?

My overwhelming memory of the Great Blackout of 2003 is lying on my back staring at more stars than I'd ever seen in my life, living for a moment in a world gone quiet, a world in which all the artificial power had shut down. And I wondered, in the starry night, who am I now?

A Time for Reflection:

This week's scripture passage talks about the importance of "wisdom." What does the word "wisdom" mean to you? Why does the scripture describe wisdom as the "tree of life" and say "those who hold her fast are called happy?" Do you think of yourself as a person who has "wisdom?"

What does it mean to be the centre of our own universes? What is the "artificial power" that blinds us? What's the problem with such a self-involved attitude? Are there some pluses as well?

What's the "metaphor of the stars?" Who are we as we stare up at a vast universe of stars?

If we are a gifted part of a "greater whole," does that call for changes in our day to day behaviour? What changes do you need to make?

Where is God in this boundless, limitless universe? What does "wisdom" tell you about God, knowing that we are tiny specks in a vast cosmos?

A Time for Prayer:

Gracious God, move us from self-involvement and selfishness to the starry, starry night of re-imagining ourselves in your image. Guide us to surrender a world of false idols which revolves around our whims and wishes. Give us the wisdom to find ourselves in service to others. Wonderful God, help us to remember, small as we are in the vast universe, that we are uniquely gifted and profoundly loved. We pray in Jesus' name, who is the Word, who is Wisdom. Amen.

A Time for Action:

I'm not the centre of the universe. I belong to God. Think, pray, and walk with God while reflecting on those two statements. Where is God taking you? When the time is right, you'll know what to do because you'll have received the gift of wisdom.

Week 43: Was "Doubting Thomas" Such a Bad Guy?

Have you ever kicked yourself for not asking the important question that was burning a hole in your brain (and stomach) throughout the course of a meeting, seminar, class, or some other gathering? You may have been wondering about this question for a long time and now here's your big chance to lay it out there, and perhaps even get a viable answer.

But, you don't do it. Something inside of you puts up a barrier and you decide to withdraw—tuck your big question away for another day; a day that will probably never come.

Have you ever wondered why? Your question may only be important to you, or it may open people up to a new way of seeing the issue at hand. But, you didn't ask it. Is there someone or something you don't trust which causes you to deny the value of your important questions?

But Thomas (who was called the Twin), one of the twelve, was not with them when Jesus came. So the other disciples told him, "We have seen the Lord." But he said to them, "Unless I see the mark of the nails in his hands, and put my finger in the mark of the nails and my hand in his side, I will not believe."

A week later his disciples were again in the house, and Thomas was with them. Although the doors were shut, Jesus came and stood among them and said, "Peace be with you." Then he said to Thomas, "Put your finger here and see my hands.

Reach out your hand and put it in my side. Do not doubt but believe." Thomas answered him, "My Lord and my God!" Jesus said to him, "Have you believed because you have seen me? Blessed are those who have not seen and yet have come to believe." (John 20: 24-29)

A Personal Journey:

The first church I ever served as a minister was in the British Columbia interior, way back in 1975. I drove from Vancouver out to the small Shuswap Lake community of Salmon Arm the night before my first Sunday service. After helping to unpack the moving van at midnight, I settled into a very uneasy sleep at about 2:00 a.m., wondering what it would be like to see all those new faces in just a few hours.

Somewhere around 3:30 a.m., the phone rang. An urgent voice on the line told me there'd been an accident on the Trans-Canada Highway, three miles east of the little village of Canoe. An ambulance was needed right away. I said I thought that was a good idea. He said something like, 'You don't understand, we need one now.' I said something like, 'Yes I do understand, you'd better call for one immediately.' He mumbled something I didn't catch, but I'm sure was unprintable, and hung up.

To make a long story short, the previous minister had been a volunteer ambulance driver and getting a call at 3:30 a.m., for him, would have made perfect sense. For me, it was baffling. But, to this day, what baffles me even more is why I didn't ask the "key question." A man calls at 3:30 a.m. asking me for advice about ambulances and I didn't ask him why. "What's going on?" I should have asked. "Why are you talking to me about ambulances at 3:30 a.m.?" But, I just, more or less, let it slide.

Dean Salter

The reason I raise this unfortunate episode is, lately, I've been wondering if our society is becoming as numbed out as I was that night back in 1975. Is our society unwilling or unable to ask key questions about faith, justice, human rights, war, and peace? Are we just muddling along, assuming (or perhaps not even caring) that somebody in power has got it figured out? Has our society become so dangerous we're now afraid to ask tough questions? Is it too risky?

The biblical figure of Thomas has been much-maligned over the centuries. "Doubting Thomas" needed to see the marks of crucifixion on the risen Christ before he could believe. His questioning, while not helping his reputation very much, nevertheless helped to demonstrate the reality of the risen Christ and that is a source of faith for countless millions. Because Thomas had questions, we all saw something important.

Why is it such a horrible misstep to ask questions of God? Why is it so awful to have doubts? Do we understand God to be such an ineffectual character that he or she isn't capable of giving us intelligent responses to our questions and doubts? If we don't bring our questions and doubts to God, aren't we betraying a lack of trust? Better to believe what we're told than to push our faith to a new level with God's help.

The fear of asking key questions isn't reserved for the sphere of religious faith. For example, do we fully understand why our forces are fighting and dying in Afghanistan? Do we understand why our country has chosen not to meet our Kyoto targets for greenhouse gas emissions (or chosen not to try, really)? Do we understand why the Douglas Creek standoff in Caledonia is into its second year with no resolution in sight? Do we understand why people wander our streets homeless and hungry? Do we understand why health care and education in this country remain grossly underfunded?

If we can't or won't ask key questions does it mean that we don't trust our society to work? Do we not believe that there should be answers—good, honest, fair answers?

In the last analysis, we could all take a good lesson from "Doubting Thomas." If we want to know the answer, we've got to ask the question. If we want the truth, we need to push for it. We need to see what's genuine and real and hold onto it. We can't do that by sleepily acknowledging, as I did long ago, that an ambulance might be a good idea. We need to ask what's going on and not be satisfied until there's a good answer.

A Time for Reflection:

How do you feel about "Doubting Thomas?" If you were to sing the virtues of Thomas, what would you say about him? If you were to criticize him, what would you say?

Do you think it's "OK" or "not OK" to have doubts about your Christian faith? Why do you feel that way? Back in Week 16 we talked about the need for hope and faith in the context of "Doubting Thomas." How do questioning and doubt fit in with the need for hope and faith? Are they mutually exclusive concepts?

When you have the "important question" in your mind, what do you do with it? Do you ask it more often than not? Do you hold back more often than not? If you hold back, why? Is it a trust issue? Who or what do you not trust? How do you feel when you hold back your important questions?

Do you think people ask enough good questions about the world we live in? If not, why are we so reticent to ask questions about the key issues of our day? What holds us back from asking our questions about such issues as Afghanistan, Kyoto, Caledonia, homelessness, hunger, health care, and education?

What happens to a society in which there are no Doubting Thomases?

A Time for Prayer:

Gracious God, teach us how to honour our questions and respect our doubts. Give us the faith, love, and trust to lay our questions and doubts before you and listen for your guidance, help, and hope. Open us, God, to believing in the gift of our own intelligence. Guide us to use that gift in pursuit of truth, justice, and peace in a world that is quickly losing touch with their meaning. In Christ's name we pray. Amen.

A Time for Action:

Promise yourself that the next time you have an "important question" to ask, you will not allow any "barriers" to deter you. Your question has value for you, and likely for others, and it belongs "out on the table" and not burning an anxious hole in your stomach. Don't just promise it. When the time comes, do it.

Week 44: Cut the Meat

When you ask people what they like about their church, the answer often comes down to a question of friendliness. A happy camper will say, "The church welcomed me; it made me feel at home." People will also speak well of the minister and the way he or she brings off Sunday worship. They'll like the social activities and one or two of the church's programs. Together, these friendly people will make up the core of the church.

But, is that enough? What constitutes a church, anyway? How is it different than a social club? While not knocking the importance of friendliness and acceptance to a church, they don't really constitute a mission. What does it mean for a church today to *genuinely* merit a title like "the Body of Christ?"

When he came to Nazareth, where he had been brought up, he went to the synagogue on the Sabbath day, as was his custom. He stood up to read, and the scroll of the prophet Isaiah was given to him. He unrolled the scroll and found the place where it was written: "The Spirit of the Lord is upon me, because he has anointed me to bring good news to the poor. He has sent me to proclaim release to the captives and recovery of sight to the blind, to let the oppressed go free, to proclaim the year of the Lord's favor."

And he rolled up the scroll, gave it back to the attendant, and sat down. The eyes of all in the synagogue were fixed on him. Then he began to say to them, "Today this scripture has been fulfilled in your hearing." (Luke 4: 16-21)

A Personal Journey:

A few years ago, I was invited to share a meal with some friends.

The table was beautifully set and the food supply seemed to stream endlessly out of the kitchen on newly-polished silver trays. I was amazed, and a little overwhelmed, by the enormous bounty on the table. Then, when I thought the table might collapse from the weight of all those trays, the chief cook brought out THE ROAST, a huge slab of beef that was lowered into the last available space, close to my chair.

When everyone was seated around the table, the chief cook/host looked earnestly at me, the only clergy-type present, and asked, "Dean, would you do the honours?" I immediately bowed my head and prayed a mighty prayer, commensurate, I thought, with the grandeur of the table and the size of THE ROAST. It went very well. When I finished, proud of my own efforts, the host gave me an odd look and said, "That was very nice, Dean, but I actually meant would you do the honour of cutting the meat!"

It strikes me that this little faux pas actually symbolizes something much more important. It symbolizes how Christian churches (and perhaps other faith communities as well) sometimes stereotype ourselves. We box ourselves in. We look upon ourselves as powerless, peripheral groups in the community whose only role is to provide a good prayer or worship service when called upon. When we accept this stereotype, we lose any sense of having a genuine mission to God's world. There's only a repetitive set of activities that are focused primarily on ourselves. If we box ourselves in, there's a real danger that we're going to consistently fail our wider community. We'll want to pray while our city, our country, and our world need us to "cut the meat."

Rev. Bill Easum is a respected consultant, in the U.S. and Canada, on the revitalization and transformation of local congregations. His message is clear and consistent: the local church has a responsibility, given its commitment to Jesus Christ, to both pray and "cut the meat."

At a recent conference in Baltimore, Easum told 450 participants from across the Christian faith spectrum that "transforming the city is much more important than building the church." Churches that focus inward on themselves, churches that work solely at perfecting their repetitive set of activities in order to please their members, are doomed to fail.

Easum says, far from placing ourselves in the backwater of community life, the churches need to rediscover a common mission. They must answer a key question: "How can all the churches in the city work together to change our city?"

The faith communities of this city—of any town or city—can be a tremendous force for good if we refuse to be isolated and boxed in. Great things can be done if we refuse to stereotype ourselves as peripheral to community life and if we refuse to become self-absorbed. If we care about transforming the city, then we'll form the partnerships to bring it about. If we substitute a passion for mission in place of our fear for survival, then the faith community is true to its calling.

In the end if, as Christians, we just want to pray, then there's great power in genuine prayer. But, to be the church, to follow Christ's call to discipleship, requires a deep sense of mission. To transform the city, it seems clear we're called to say a powerful prayer and then work in partnership to "cut the meat" with all the skill and ability we can muster.

A Time for Reflection:

What do you think are the main things that most people like and dislike about their local churches?

What do you see as the similarities and differences between the Christian church as "social club" and the Christian church as "the Body of Christ?" Where does your local church fit in this comparison?

Why do local churches often stereotype themselves as being peripheral to the life of their communities? Are we more content to pray "on cue" than to take leadership in changing our communities? Do we sacrifice mission for comfort? Are we happy to stay boxed in?

Discuss Jesus' proclamation in the synagogue at Nazareth. What was he saying about his ministry? What does this passage say about "the Body of Christ?" Read a bit further. How did people react?

"Transforming the city is much more important than building the church." What does it mean to have a clear mission about which you are *passionate*? What impact can such a mission have on yourself, the community, and the church? Do you think transforming the city is incompatible with building the church?

A Time for Prayer:

Loving God, help us to understand what it means to be the Body of Christ in this world. Help us, as churches, to reach outward with a passionate mission for the poor, the hurting, and the disadvantaged. May we find in you the power to transform our towns and cities into true communities, making our churches partners in authentic change rather than social clubs for the slightly wounded. Gracious God, we share in the dynamic ministry of Jesus, and for this honour we celebrate your holy name. Amen.

A Time for Action:

If God's call to the Body of Christ today is to "transform the city" what exactly does that mean in your situation? Connect with one or two mission-oriented people in your congregation and brainstorm what three or four programs or projects would be important "steps in the journey" towards transforming your town or city. Are people isolated? Are youth at risk? Are family violence, unemployment, or the plight of immigrants an issue in your town? Pick a mission about which you feel passionate, develop a team, create a plan, form partnerships, and take critical actions to transform your community. Understand that your mission is also your way of honouring the power of Christ in your life.

Week 45: The Mentor's Gift

Many of us aren't overly confident people. We may have lived a considerable number of years, enjoying some wonderful victories and enduring some shattering losses, but we still feel we have little advice to give the world. And yet, our faith is stubbornly demanding in this regard. Scripture calls us never to hide our lamp under a bushel basket. It challenges us to experience our world as "neighbours" and share from the depths of what God has given us.

Our emotions may urge us to curl up within ourselves and hold the world at arms length. But, our God expects and demands more of us. Our God calls us to share our gifts in community—to mentor and to be mentored in order to grow the "kingdom." There seems little question about the call. The question lies in our response.

You are the light of the world. A city built on a hill cannot be hid. No one after lighting a lamp puts it under the bushel basket, but on the lampstand, and it gives light to all in the house. In the same way, let your light shine before others, so that they may see your good works and give glory to your Father in heaven. (Matthew 5: 14-16)

A Personal Journey:

When I was a teenager I was, to put it kindly, "directionally challenged." I had an unfortunate knack for getting lost on every new journey, no matter how clear and detailed the directions might be. If there was a dead end, I'd find it. If there was a street the mapmaker couldn't imagine including in the directions, I'd be on it.

So it was no surprise that one Saturday night, while trying to find a classmate named Mary Pat for a first date, I became hopelessly lost. After a lengthy search involving much of our small town, I stumbled onto the right street, hopelessly late, and drove up to the large brick bungalow described in the directions. For some reason, our high school principal, Mr. Kenney, opened the door and after an awkward moment he invited me to come in and sit on the couch.

Also for some reason, it never occurred to me to ask Mr. Kenney why he was living at the O'Neill's house. Within a minute or two Mr. Kenney emerged from the kitchen with two lemonades. He sat in the chair opposite to me and asked how I was doing; was everything going OK at school, was there anything he could do to help? He was such a warm and kindly man I wanted to assure him that, apart from all the academic requirements, school was fine.

After a respectable amount of time, I looked at the stairway behind him and asked if Mary Pat would be ready soon. Mr. Kenney smiled as if a light of recognition tripped on in his head. "Mary Pat is probably ready Dean, but not here. The O'Neills live three doors down. But, listen, you're always welcome to stop by here when you'd like to talk about something."

The point of this story (you may be wondering) doesn't have anything to do with my directional issues, which have not been cured by the passage of time. The point of this story is to introduce Mr. Kenney, who is the archetype of what it means to be a good mentor in this world. Stumbling and confused as I was, he invited me into his home. He made me feel welcome and accepted. He was totally prepared to listen to my worries and concerns and help me find my way. Even at my most ridiculous and foolish moment, Mr. Kenney didn't ridicule me. He reassured me that he was there for me if I needed him.

This "wrong way" story could easily have been about my humiliation. But, what I take from it is the grace with which my high school principal opened his door to me and his total willingness to mentor me through the "issues" I was bringing into his living room. He could have rejected me at the door. He could have said, "Sorry Dean, I'm on my own time now." But, instead of a barrier, he offered a pathway into his life and wisdom.

Mr. Kenney was a very religious man, and I wonder if his gift for mentoring was enriched by the greatest mentor of all. Jesus spent countless hours teaching his small group of disciples, talking with them, listening to their questions and fears, and equipping them for ministry. He loved them, guided them, and expected the world of them. Jesus didn't have an "off duty" switch, he had a "kingdom" switch that was always on. Mr. Kenney lived that way, too.

In a fast-paced, "me-centred" world it's easy to lose sight of the very human need we have for support, wisdom, and guidance from others. In a world where acquisition so often trumps community, it's easy to deny our support, wisdom, and guidance to those who look to us for help. It's easy to keep our own counsel.

More than ever, the world needs people like Arthur Kenney. We need mentors. We need people who will open the door, even when they're "off the clock"; people who will really listen and explore the mysteries of wisdom with searchers and seekers who are not quite lost, but not quite found.

Today, I feel quite lucky to have stumbled into my principal's house that night close to forty years ago. It gave me a chance to experience the depth of caring that goes hand in hand with a great mentor. It's a role that belongs to all of us; one we ignore at our own peril in a super-charged, self-involved world.

What happens when no one listens? What happens when wisdom and experience are never shared? In the last analysis, those who refuse to open the door can never be truly rich.

A Time for Reflection:

Describe "mentoring" as you understand it. Have you ever had a mentor or been a mentor? Describe the situation. What drew you into mentoring and how did the experience feel for you? If you've never experienced mentoring, what do you think has held you back?

What do you think are the best qualities of a successful mentor?

What do you think are some of the dangers and pitfalls of mentoring?

Why was Jesus such a good mentor? What is it about our faith that literally "calls" us into mentoring and how do we answer the call with integrity?

Why is mentoring so important in developing community? What happens when no one listens? What happens when wisdom and experience are never shared?

A Time for Prayer:

Gracious God, you have held us up in your hands of love. You have shown us the ways of Wisdom. In both our joys and sorrows you've walked beside us. You've taught us, guided us, and challenged us. We know in our hearts that you want us to reach out to others in the same loving, mentoring spirit. We hear the call. In the powerful name of Christ, may we have the courage to answer. Amen.

A Time for Action:

Read as much as you can about mentoring. Interview someone who is known as a mentor. Join a mentoring program in your church or community. If there is no program, work with others to define the parametres of such an initiative and get a mentoring program started. Also, be open to the informal opportunities for mentoring that arise on a daily basis and find faithful ways to walk with those who ask for your support.

Week 46: The Calm Before the Storm

All animals have instincts which, to a greater or lesser degree, influence their behaviour. The family retriever chases a stick into the water over and over again, grabs it gently, and brings it back to you. An alley cat spends its nights hunting the neighbourhood for its prey. Most creatures are instinctively aware of their respective mating seasons. Nobody needs to show them a calendar.

Instincts are very compelling. You don't see the family retriever stop at the edge of the water, scratch its head with a paw, and look back at its owner as if to ask, "Why am I doing this?" They just leap into the water—the first few times anyway. Human beings, with our large mass of grey matter, are supposed to be one animal capable of asking the "why" questions on a regular basis: "Why am I doing this? Why is this important?"

Humans are *capable* of asking the "why" questions. But, that doesn't mean we actually do it. Take Christmas, for example. Why do we sail into this gathering storm the same way every year? Why do we follow the traditions and practices we follow? Why do we repeat things over and over again which have lost their meaning for us? Why do we bother with this season at all? Is anybody asking these questions or do we just follow our survival instincts year after year until the "holiday season" is over?

"Surely, from now on all generations will call me blessed; for the Mighty One has done great things for me, and holy is his name. His mercy is for those who fear him from generation to generation. He has shown strength with his arm; he has scattered the proud in the thoughts of their hearts. He has brought down the powerful from their thrones, and lifted up the lowly; he has filled the hungry with good things, and sent the rich away empty." (Luke 1: 48b-53)

A Personal Journey:

I want to talk about Christmas. Yes, I know it's over a month away, but that's my point, really. This is the *time* to talk about Christmas. We're already polishing our credit cards and re-soleing our shoes for long walks in the mall. We've been testing out cookie recipes for the past six weeks. Santa Claus started to pop up on the TV before we finished carving the pumpkin at Halloween. Who knows when we'll start waking up in the night, soaked in sweat, thinking about boxes, ladders, and Christmas lights?

Oh, this is the time to talk about Christmas alright. In another week, Christmas will bury us like an avalanche. There'll be no discussing it. Tasks will have to be accomplished pronto. All the life force of the entire family will be marshalled into buying the best gifts ever, hosting the finest parties, and gracing the neighbourhood with an awesome display of lights. There will be lists upon lists of things to accomplish. If we don't talk about Christmas *right now*, it'll be too late. Once the avalanche begins, all you can do is run for your life. If you listen carefully you can already hear the rumbling in the distance.

I am not a Scrooge. I am not grouchy when it comes to Christmas. Christmas shopping, in and of itself, isn't a bad thing. Where would the economy be without it? Christmas cookies are tasty. Christmas lights are often attractive. Overall, I can see myself supporting Christmas as an economic necessity with some nice perks. But, why should I get excited about it? Is there any reason to throw myself into it, to feel passionate about it? That's what I want to know in November. I want to know why I should leap into this Christmas thing again because, you know, it *is* a lot of work.

I want to know why I'm buying Christmas gifts. Is there some positive reason behind it? Is it done as an act of love? Is there some compelling spiritual force that drives my generosity? Am I buying a gift to celebrate life or just to keep the minions happy? What does buying a gift mean to me? How does it relate to anything in my life?

I want to know why I should balance precariously on my old ladder in the freezing rain to put up Christmas lights again this year. Is it because their shining gives me, and those around me, a sense of the holy? Is it because I wish to honour the light that Jesus Christ brought into the world? Is it because in the quiet moments of a cold, crisp night I'd like to go outside and feel genuine peace, and I'd like to give that feeling to others through my Christmas lights? Or do I put them up because, well, I always put them up and what would the neighbours think if I didn't?

I want to know why I should be a joyous partyer this Christmas. Is it because I actually feel joyous? Am I happy that the spirit of Christmas is a unifying force that brings me together with family and friends and helps me to value them rather than take them for granted? Or do I party because, well, it's expected?

All things considered, I think November is a wonderful time to think about Christmas. Particularly, we might want to think about it if the celebration is getting harder and more strained each year—if it's draining us rather than energizing us. We might want to ask the "why" question. Why am I doing what I'm doing? Is there something positive and life-giving that I've lost touch with? Where's the spiritual centre of this season for me? What do I need to give up, add, alter, or change in order to celebrate Christmas this year?

Consider it now. Time's not on our side. The avalanche is moments away from sweeping us down the hill. Who has time to think when that happens?

A Time for Reflection:

How does "the Christmas season" make you feel? Discuss all the emotions— positive, negative, and in-between—that the season draws out of you. Why such a variety of emotions?

This week's scripture is an excerpt from the "Magnificat of Mary" (Mary's Song of Praise). Do you think "the Christmas season" would be different if this passage was considered the heart of the celebration? How would things be different? Would it be a positive change or not?

Are there Christmas practices or traditions that you'd like to drop because they've lost their meaning for you? What stands in the way of dropping them?

Are there Christmas practices that you'd like to begin in order to make the season more meaningful to you? What stands in the way of adopting them?

Does your celebration of Christmas, overall, serve to enhance your faith or are you just as happy to see it as a commercial event and let it go at that? If it enhances your faith, how do you make that happen?

A Time for Prayer:

Loving God, as Christmas approaches this year, help me to walk with you and learn exactly why the birth of your son needs to take hold of my spirit. Help me to understand why this season changes everything and guide me to grow my faith so I clearly know the difference between trappings and truth when I look at the Christ Child. Amen.

A Time for Action:

It's difficult to change everything at once. Instead, choose one Christmas practice or tradition this year that you think has lost its meaning. Discuss it with your family, if appropriate, and, if there's consensus, drop it for this year. At the same time suggest one new Christmas practice that you believe would make the season more meaningful. Once again, if appropriate, discuss it with your family and, if there's consensus, try it for this year. Be open to the possibility that others may have ideas about what they'd like to drop or add as well, but be sure you have your ideas developed as a clear starting point.

Week 47: An Attitude of Gratitude

There are any number of ways to define ourselves in this world. Let me suggest two. So much of day to day life boils down to whether we perceive ourselves as people of "entitlement" or people of "gratitude." If we're constantly concerned with obtaining our "fair share" of the world's goods and services; if we believe, in essence, that the world owes us a quantity of its abundance, then we are people of entitlement. If we understand the world around us as God's "gift" then our worldview changes dramatically. We are no longer concerned with "our fair share," since there is no "fair share" to think about. If what we have is "gift" then our response in the great world is to live a life of gratitude rather than acquisition. The footprints of entitlement and gratitude are as different as night and day. The question for each of us is where do we stand on the pathway between these two worldviews?

I hate, I despise your festivals, and I take no delight in your solemn assemblies. Even though you offer me your burnt offerings and grain offerings, I will not accept them; and the offerings of well-being of your fatted animals I will not look upon. Take away from me the noise of your songs; I will not listen to the melody of your harps. But let justice roll down like waters, and righteousness like an ever-flowing stream. (Amos 5: 21-24)

A Personal Journey:

I never asked my parents about this, but I suspect that I wasn't the easiest child to raise back in the 1950s and early 1960s. As a young boy in the seemingly abundant post-war years you simply had to have the right things in order to fit in with the right crowd. Without these things—a good bike, a respectable ball glove, a quality lunch pail (preferably Roy Rogers), a short jacket, a well-shaped ball cap, etc. etc. etc.—you might as well stay home. Even though my parents were far from wealthy, I fully expected them to provide "the right stuff," the stuff that would make me socially acceptable.

Even given this need for "the right stuff" you cannot imagine the abject carrying on I perpetrated on my poor parents one long-ago Christmas morning when they bought the wrong board hockey set. Oh the calamity! On this board, the players were fixed in place where the proper set allowed them to slide back and forth. Tears flooded down my face. "This is the wrong one," I remember screaming, my face contorted in horror and anguish. "How could you buy this piece of crap!" I was inconsolable for the rest of the day. How could I go on? Can there be life after being presented with "the wrong stuff?"

Looking back on that event, I think my parents should have duct-taped that hockey set to my back and tossed me out into the snow. But, of course, they didn't. Two days later, my dad went back to the store and bought the "right" one and all of a sudden the world was a better place again. I had whined my way to the prize.

I try not to feel too much guilt over my childhood. In spite of what my sister says, I'm sure I must have had some positive moments—even for a bratty kid. But, to this day, I do feel guilty about the board hockey incident on Christmas morning. Of all the times to have a daylong conniption, Christmas day is a poor choice. To buy gifts, people have, in most cases, made great sacrifices of time and money, in keeping with the loving and generous spirit of Christmas. They have put themselves out in order to make others feel happy and cared about. Even if the gift isn't "great" it's still a gift, given with a good spirit.

Personally, I've come to think that the only acceptable feeling on Christmas day is a feeling of gratitude. Not only do we have the greatest gift of all, the Christ Child, to celebrate, we also have other presents that come to us unearned and (dare I say) undeserved. Why in God's name would you have a conniption over a freely offered present? Just smile and find out the return policy.

There's a lot to be said for gratitude, and not just at Christmas time. Some years ago the United Church had a fundraising slogan which encouraged people to have "an attitude of gratitude." I think it should be more of a life slogan. An attitude of gratitude moves us beyond the yawning pit of entitlement, the need to "grab my share and run," and into a world of giftedness. Ultimately, the question becomes 'Does the world owe me the things I want or does God call me to live abundantly through the gifts I've been given?' Entitlement is a battle that tears the life out of people and has them babbling things like, "I'm entitled to my entitlements." Their life force is spent collecting their fair share, which by definition is never enough. Those who live with gratitude are aware that all of creation is a gift and God's call is to spend our life force in balance with humanity and all of nature. Through gratitude, we understand that there is no balance without fairness and justice. Through gratitude, we know that there is no balance when people are enslaved. Gratitude is the energy through which a broken world is healed.

In retrospect, I suppose it would be a lot to ask of a bratty little kid like me to show some gratitude on that hyped up Christmas morning long ago. I didn't grasp the concept. But, I was lucky that as one Christmas led to another I had parents and other role models who quietly taught me through words and actions what it meant to have an attitude of gratitude. They could have given me no greater gift.

A Time for Reflection:

In our scripture passage for this week, what is the prophet Amos saying to people about what's important in life and what it means to truly worship God?

Discuss the role of "entitlement" in the world today. Do you think there's a justifiable place for it?

Discuss the role of "gratitude" in the world today. How does it (or could it) shape the world we live in?

Where would you place yourself on the pathway between entitlement and gratitude right now in your life? Why do you place yourself where you do? Are you happy there or do you want to be in a different place? If so, how will you get there?

If what we have is a gift from God, how, specifically, would you like to say "thank you" today?

A Time for Prayer:

Gracious God, we thank you for the gift of abundant life which you offer freely to all humankind. We are sorry for our grasping sense of entitlement which has left so many with so little. In our sin, we have pushed your world out of balance and turned our backs on you, showing hardness of heart where gratitude belongs. Forgive us, we pray. Guide us to live in Christ and finally understand the true nature of gift. Amen.

A Time for Action:

Based on the questions above, make a list of the specific things you want to do (this week, this month, this year) that will clearly show your gratitude to God for all the gifts you've received. Make a firm commitment and set a plan which will allow you to "live out" your list.

Dean Salter

Week 48: Where Is the Common Decency?

I made a little mistake the other day. I was running around doing a variety of errands and my last stop was the grocery store. In my fevered state, I caught sight of someone leaving a good parking spot near the entrance. A good parking spot at Christmas time is like a nice, juicy steak to most of us, so I dollied right in as soon as I could. What I didn't see was that another car, on the other side, had been waiting for the spot. I'm not the sweetest soul in the world but fair is fair and I felt guilty enough that I was actually prepared to back out again and let him have the treasured parking spot. But, before I could do anything, the driver started carrying on like I'd burned down his house and kidnapped his mother. The fist was shaking, the horn was blowing, and he was mouthing obscenities while giving me "the look of death." Within a few seconds he hit the gas and peeled off to find another spot. This little incident is now "a memory of Christmas" for me. I wonder why things couldn't have gone better. What was missing in each of us that created such a scene? To be honest, once he blew up at me, I lost all desire "to do the right thing."

"You are the salt of the earth; but if salt has lost its taste, how can its saltiness be restored? It is no longer good for anything, but is thrown out and trampled under foot." (Matthew 5:13)

261

A Personal Journey:

Some years ago, I was at a conference that I can't remember anything about in terms of content. It was held in a distant city I've also forgotten. But, apart from these little gaps, it will always stand for me as a very memorable event.

It was memorable for the after-hours gatherings where people socialized well into the evening. Those were the places to meet interesting people and learn interesting things.

At one such gathering, the host, a noted professor, spent the entire evening with his back to the crowd, working on his laptop computer. People seemed to accept his behaviour as nothing more than an amusing peccadillo. 'Old Professor So and So is off in his own little world again.'

Maybe I'm too grouchy these days but I think of that professor's actions as rude. There's nothing so desperately critical in the work of most professors that they have blanket permission to disobey the rules of common courtesy.

A recent poll conducted in the United States by Associated Press-Ipsos found that 70 per cent of Americans believe people are ruder today than they were 20 or 30 years ago. And, after facing daily episodes of road rage, line-cutting, biting comments from people we don't even know, and the obsessive, inappropriate use of communications gadgets, who among us will argue with them?

Peggy Newfield, founder of a self-help group called Personal Best, blames parents for the upturn in bad behaviour—particularly those parents who came of age in the wild, informal 1960s and 1970s. They are somewhat clueless when it comes to stressing the importance of good manners, she says. And, the media "pours it on" with its daily parade of ill-mannered celebrities.

At the risk of sounding rude—so what? Does it really matter that we're living in an increasingly ill-mannered and desensitized world? After all, we're healthier and wealthier than we've ever been. We live in a world of countless possibilities and opportunities. Why grouse about a little dive in the state of our manners or a small decline in our ability to offer common courtesies?

If history is any judge, perhaps we should worry. Joe Schlesinger, a former CBC foreign correspondent, spent his high-powered career reporting on violent, dysfunctional governments and societies around the world. He saw a common thread in the horrors he witnessed. In his memoir, *Time Zones*, he writes, "Decency had for too long been missing from politics and diplomacy. Everyone was chasing after higher, more important goals—progress, prosperity, peace, or just power—to pay attention to plain decency, that banal amalgam of common courtesy, compassion, and consideration, of moderation and generosity."

We set aside plain decency at our own risk. What value do all our possibilities and opportunities have if we don't see them through the eyes and the actions of Schlesinger's plain decency? Where are we headed as a society without it?

As we enter into the Christmas season, there'll be a surfeit of attention paid to the venerable notions of hope, peace, joy, and love. A lot of attention, I might say, but precious little action. The words have become iconic, taking on a shining, ethereal quality right up to December 25, and then vapourizing on Boxing Day.

Hope, peace, joy, and love have become more of a seasonal tradition than a day to day reality. These four icons surround the Christmas season at the same time that resentments boil in our heads about traffic jams and stolen parking spots. They don't stop us from cutting in line or disrupting family gatherings or pageants with bleating cellphones. They fail to mitigate our ongoing hatreds and prejudices.

Rather than failing to achieve hope, peace, joy, and love again this Christmas, perhaps we should strive for something less tinsel-like in daily life.

It's not acceptable to blithely wander down the path of a desensitized and increasingly ill-mannered world. We've already seen the imponderable human cost of following that road. If we take steps in the other direction, in the direction of plain decency, perhaps one day our seasonal icons of hope, peace, joy, and love will be released from the studied "sweetness" of the Christmas season and we'll discover their truths in the roughness and struggles of daily life.

A Time for Reflection:

How would you have handled the parking lot incident described in this week's introduction? What's at stake in this type of situation?

Do you agree with the American poll that expresses a general sense that people are ruder today than two or three decades ago? How have you experienced rudeness? What do you think of Peggy Newfield's explanation?

In his memoir, Joe Schlesinger wrote, "Decency had for too long been missing from politics and diplomacy." Discuss the term "decency" as used by Schlesinger. Do you think "decency" is a key factor in politics and diplomacy today? Why do you think "decency" is such a hard concept for many nations? For many people?

Do you agree that "hope," "peace," "joy," and "love" are the "sweet words" of the Christmas season which have largely lost their meaning? If so, how can their "stronger," more genuine meanings be regained?

What does it mean in real terms to be "the salt of the earth" as followers of Jesus? How does such a call to action make you feel? Do you feel daunted? Is there grace in this call?

A Time for Prayer:

Hopeful, peaceful, joyous, and loving God, help us to keep hold of the common decency that's central to our faith. Guide us to a respect and kindness towards others that's borne from the great reality that Christ is in our hearts. If we are aggressive, may it be in the desire to heal the sick and work beside the disadvantaged. If we are bold, may it be in the desire to advance the peaceable kingdom. May we discover the power of our convictions, but may we first discover the decency. Amen.

A Time for Action:

Think less about hope, peace, joy, and love in the build-up to Christmas this year and think more about living in Christ and meeting the day to day experiences of your life with common decency.

Week 49: K.I.S.S.

Most of us have grown up in a world that continues to be very "me-centred." So much of our daily lives revolves around what I'm doing, how I'm doing, and what I can do to improve myself. It's not surprising that, when it comes to celebrating Christmas at church, the focus is once again on "me." Rather than focus on what God has done in the gift of the Christ Child, we focus on creating the best, bang-up, top-of-the-line, entertaining worship services we can muster. Certainly, we must create something that's light years better than last year or what's the point of celebrating at all?

Does our desire to create a new and improved worship extravaganza every Christmas prove our faith or does it mean we take ourselves more seriously than we take our God? Is it possible God just wants us to K.I.S.S. (Keep It Simple Stupid) and think more profoundly about what it means for the Word to become flesh?

When you are praying, do not heap up empty phrases as the Gentiles do; for they think that they will be heard because of their many words. Do not be like them, for your Father knows what you need before you ask him. (Matthew 6: 7-8)

A Personal Journey:

Before I semi-retired a couple of years ago, I spent 27 years working as an ordained minister in The United Church of Canada. Some years were served in the church bureaucracy and some years were served in the pastorate. Lots of interesting times; lots of challenges over the years. But, I'd have to say that some of the greatest, most persistent struggles I had during my "pastoral" years centred around Christmas.

I realize that the optics of a Christian minister struggling with Christmas aren't good. And, in fact, I have no moral, ethical, or theological problems with celebrating Christmas. I like Christmas! Really! At a very fundamental level it does my heart good to celebrate the birth of the Christ Child year after year.

The problems I had with Christmas were always centred on worship. How do you make Christmas worship as wondrous as the event itself? What new and interesting ways can you find to perk up the Christmas services and help people see the old, old story in a grand new light? How do you set off the fireworks that should surround our celebration of Christmas?

There's a lot of angst involved for worship planners when they're always trying to create a richer, deeper, and more meaningful Christmas celebration this year than last. If Celine Dion stopped by to sing "O Holy Night" at the Christmas Eve service last year, what do you do this year? Can you go back to Bertie Buckle's less than heavenly rendition of "Angels from the Realms of Glory?" No, of course not. You can only follow Celine by bringing in the Mormon Tabernacle Choir. If you don't do something spectacular, people will most certainly lose their Christmas spirit and become morbidly depressed.

Some years ago, in one of my pastoral charges, I totally succumbed to the "extravaganza" school of Christmas worship. On Christmas Eve we threw in every unique twist and turn you could possibly mix together in public worship. We sang every Christmas hymn ever written. We had a dynamic one-act play which sprawled across the stage like a Hollywood epic. We had solos, instrumentals, duets, and choir anthems. We had a full sermon followed by communion and we ended the production with candlelighting and a solemn rendition of "Silent Night."

Unfortunately, our Christmas Eve extravaganza clocked in at slightly over two hours and thirty minutes. It was not a success. The downcast worshippers who filed past me just before midnight looked as if they'd just completed a marathon. Wordlessly, they wandered into the snowy night.

One of the last people to pump my hand was one of our most unshakably positive and supportive members. She looked me in the eye and said, "Next year, Dean, lets go back to carols and readings and leave it at that, OK?"

It was her way of saying K.I.S.S.— "Keep It Simple Stupid!" And that was a lesson I needed to learn. Christmas worship isn't about our ability to put together a great show. It isn't about trying to top ourselves each year with more and better features. Christmas is about the gift of the Christ Child to all of humanity—the Word of God taking on human form and living among us. It's about a love so unique, inclusive, and encompassing that it came to us in the raw simplicity of a stable.

There's a danger that spectacular Christmas worship may be more about us than God. It sometimes feels as if our only goal is to top ourselves, put on a better show than last year. But, isn't the Christmas event wonderful enough without all the choreography we add to it? Why can't we just keep our celebrations simple? Why don't we just tell the story with love and let God do the rest?

A Time for Reflection:

What do Christmas worship services mean to you? What do you want from them as a person of faith?

What specific aspects of Christmas worship have the most meaning for you? Why?

What specific aspects of Christmas worship have the least meaning for you? Why?

How do we go about planning Christmas worship which is sharp, thoughtful, creative, and centred in the desire to know God and listen to God? Why is this a difficult goal?

How would you apply the K.I.S.S. principle to Christmas worship? To other aspects of church life?

A Time for Prayer:

Loving God, guide us to make this Christmas more about you than it is about us. Guide us to worry less about making our celebrations of the Christ Child bigger and better and more about celebrating what the Word made flesh means to a bruised and broken world. We ask our prayer in the name of that same Christ Child who continues to hold hope, peace, joy, and love up to the mirror of our world. Amen.

A Time for Action:

With the K.I.S.S. principle in mind, join the planning team which is working on your Christmas worship services. Work with them to answer the questions above and develop your worship services accordingly.

Week 50: The One Perfect Thing About Christmas

Why is it that mental health practitioners have to work overtime during the Christmas season? What is it about Christmas, in particular, that causes many average citizens such compelling, nearly debilitating angst? It's not, after all, an unhappy concept. Christmas is fundamentally about birth—new life and new hope. In and of itself, that seems like a good thing; not something that should send us running to our friendly neighbourhood psychologists. So why the bother? What are we bringing to this season that doesn't belong there? Have we created a false celebration that's, at its heart, more about us than it is about God; more about our striving for recognition than it is about recognizing the Christ Child? If Christmas is about pretending and perfection it's a dangerous ride for all of us. If it's about a cold, unclean stable and the birth of hope then we need to put down the tinsel and find out why.

And the Word became flesh and dwelt among us, and we have seen his glory, the glory as of a father's only son, full of grace and truth...From his fullness we have all received, grace upon grace. The law indeed was given through Moses; grace and truth came through Jesus Christ. No one has ever seen God. It is God the only Son, who is close to the Father's heart, who has made him known. (John 1:14 and 16-18)

A Personal Journey:

Have you acknowledged in your heart of hearts that you're not perfect?

OK, sure, you've paid lip service to the idea. But, have you really accepted the idea deep down inside where the brain waves flash and the blood pumps?

This whole notion of not being perfect has serious and disturbing consequences. It means we must acknowledge that not everything we say or do is brilliant or ideal...or even right! It means that we sometimes make wrong choices and head down dimly-lit roads that culminate with a big "DEAD END." Imperfection can be extremely messy and somewhere deep in our psyche we know that our parents wouldn't approve. But, it's the path we walk day by day.

The corollary to being imperfect is the even more disturbing fact that we're not going to be perfect anytime soon. In fact, if history is our window to the future, there's no reason to believe that humanity will ever be perfect.

I, myself, struggled with this notion for a while. As a young man, imperfection wasn't an option. I could never be wrong! But, over the years, a great body of evidence was built up and it dawned on me that I wasn't genetically disposed towards perfection. Not at all. Nor was anyone else. It just isn't a real possibility, although there's always a nagging pull.

We're imperfect people living in an imperfect world. Just look at the front page of any daily newspaper. Pick any day and you'll read a sad litany of information about terrorist attacks, ballistic missiles, crime, discrimination, injustice, racism, and ongoing wars in Iraq and Afghanistan. Of course, there's happier news. Of course, the headlines tend to blare out the more horrific, strange, and unusual events of the day. But, the point is, there is nothing "perfect" about our world.

So, if we're imperfect and we live in an imperfect world, why is it that we strive so mightily to create 'the perfect Christmas?' We hustle and dodge through countless stores looking for the perfect gifts. We search for the perfect tree. We lay out the perfect decorations, perfectly. We prepare the perfect cookies and cook the perfect meal. We expect the perfect conversations with friends and relations. We listen for the perfect shouts of satisfaction when the presents are opened.

Now, I'm not a 'humbug' when it comes to Christmas. In fact, I enjoy the season. I think the gift-giving, the hustle and bustle, the tree, the decorations, the food, and the fellowship are wonderful. But, clearly, it will not be perfect. It *cannot* be perfect. The truth is, we need to let go of 'the perfect Christmas.' It's a kind of neurotic illusion that has always created far more angst than joy.

Let me say it again with emphasis: **We need to let go of the perfect Christmas.** And, if we can let it go, we may be able to make space for something much more special and much more vital. Doesn't the real joy of Christmas reside in the fact that "God so loved the world?" The perfect thing we celebrate at Christmas is God's love. We celebrate the fact that God accepts us and loves us, with all of our imperfections, and wants us to experience abundant life in ways we have yet to imagine.

It's not about hellfire and damnation. It's not about being perfect 'or else.' It's about God—the God who "so loved the world" that he (or she) showed us the face of abundance and painted a picture of life, love, and relationship that we'd never seen before.

We're not perfect and we're not going to be perfect. What's important at Christmas is to understand that we are perfectly loved.

A Time for Reflection:

If Christmas is about a cold, unclean stable and the birth of hope, then how should it be celebrated? Are we doing the things we need to do in order to genuinely "feel" Christmas in a spiritual way? What should we hang onto in celebrating Christmas? What should we let go of? Why is it so hard to let go of things we've "always done?"

What is it about Christmas that activates all our anxieties about "perfection?" Most of us realize that we're not perfect. But, is perfection actually a goal to strive for? Is there something else we should be striving for? What's wrong with trying to find the perfect tree or to bake the perfect cookies?

What does it mean to you to say that "the Word became flesh and dwelt among us?" Why is that important to you? To others? To the world?

Christmas isn't about what *we* do, it's about what *God* does. What does this statement mean to you?

We're not perfect and we're not going to be perfect. What's important at Christmas is to understand that we are perfectly loved by God. How close does your Christmas celebration come to celebrating this truth?

A Time for Prayer:

Loving God, help me to understand that the world doesn't revolve around my anxieties and my prideful strivings to do those things you've not given me to do and to be those things you've not given me to be. Gracious God, open me totally to the guiding power of your perfect love. Help me to feel and understand my gifts and to joyously exercise them in the world as one who truly understands that they come from the heart of God. At Christmas, may I not celebrate what *I* can do but, rather, what *you* have done and continue to do each day from your abundance. Amen.

A Time for Action:

Christmas isn't about being perfect. It's about being perfectly loved by God. Make a list of all the things in your celebration of Christmas that help to carry the spirit of this statement. Do you need to add something? Make this list the centerpiece of Christmas. Make a list of all the things which are "neutral". Keep what you enjoy and discard the rest. Make a list of all the things in your celebration of Christmas that work against the above statement. De-emphasize or discard them. Do the best you can to minimize their impact. Build a Christmas this year that's focused on God's love and how the Word of God gives abundant life.

Week 51: Deeper Than the Shopping Malls

It's important to recognize that Christmas is about God's love for us and for the world around us. But, the word "love" sometimes gets a little too mushy with overuse. It's trotted out as the solution to virtually every problem, with little thought given to how anything actually gets done.

God's love is not mushy. God's love, as we understand it from scripture, is nothing short of "radical." In this love, injustice must be challenged and authority and ancient patterns of thought must be judged in the light of Christ's lordship. In this love, there is preferential concern for the poor and disadvantaged and divisions among neighbours must be healed. God's radical love often runs counter to the popular culture, and those who practice this love will find themselves unloved by the powers that be in this world. It's a love that's born of the radical gift of the Christ Child to humanity and it issues less in words than it does in actions.

In that region there were shepherds living in the fields, keeping watch over their flocks by night. Then an angel of the Lord stood before them, and the glory of the Lord shone around them, and they were terrified. But the angel said to them, "Do not be afraid; for see—I am bringing you good news of great joy for all the people: to you is born this day in the city of David a Saviour, who is the Messiah, the Lord." (Luke 2: 8-11)

A Personal Journey:

With all the hype around Christmas, you wonder if it makes sense anymore as a religious holiday.

It certainly makes sense as a commercial holiday. Families will spend over $800 this year on Christmas gifts. Canada Post will enjoy a seasonal spike of 20 percent in mail delivery—good for the bottom line. Without Christmas, our whole economy would end the year as flat as a pancake. If we didn't have Christmas, we'd probably have to invent it just to keep the engine of commerce alive and well.

But, does it make sense as a religious holiday? In a multicultural country like Canada, Christmas isn't celebrated as a religious holiday by a significant cross-section of society. On top of that, there are large numbers of citizens who don't adhere to any faith. Christmas is a holiday break, but it doesn't hold religious importance for them.

There will be many this year for whom Christmas will be a massive personal struggle. It will be the first Christmas without a loved one. Marriages and families have split up since last Christmas. Sickness and unemployment weigh more heavily at this time of year. Far from being a great religious event, many people view Christmas as something to be survived.

Christmas may be a commercial success again this year, but has it become something of a chronic religious failure?

The answer, I suppose, is both 'yes' and 'no.' The commercial locomotive has certainly taken the season over—to a degree that there's little room left for religious expression. It's a year-end holiday for most people, even if many would like it to mean something more in their lives.

But, at another level, Christmas doesn't look like a religious failure at all. At another level, the season really can't fail and using the word "failure" seems totally inappropriate.

Christmas is fundamentally about birth. Birth is about confidence and hope. It's about renewal and regeneration. Birth is about the courage to go on; to multiply and progress.

The birth of the Christ Child is a powerful symbol that the world doesn't need to be ruled by our basest values. It symbolizes that we have the potential to live in a world ruled by dynamic, healing, and radical love. This is a hope shared by all the world's great religions. It's a hope shared by those who flock to Christmas Eve services every year.

In the end, Christmas succeeds because it can reach us at a deeper level than the shopping malls. Christmas succeeds because it has the power to reach into that part of us that hopes and dreams and wants to take positive action in the world. And, that's a part of ourselves that we genuinely want and need to explore.

A Time for Reflection:

What do you see as the fundamental differences between God's radical love and the way our society understands "love?"

Why do you think the birth of Jesus is announced in such a dramatic way to a group of shepherds? Why wouldn't the angels go directly to the political and religious leaders of the day to share their "news?"

What portion of your Christmas celebration would you say is "commercial" and what portion is "religious?" Why does it work out this way? Do you wish the percentages could be changed?

Finish this sentence: "I celebrate Christmas because....." Discuss why you finished the sentence the way you did.

The bottom line is that Christmas can never be called a failure. In your own words, explain what Christmas brings into your life as a person of faith.

What is this birth all about? Explain what it brings into the life of the world.

A Time for Prayer:

Loving God, my Christmas list is long and there are long hours of preparation ahead. There is much to be done. I pray that what happens in my house over the next few hours and days will create happiness and draw people together. Where there's joy we'll feel your presence. Gracious God, empower me, I pray, to place one thing at the top of my Christmas list. One thing that shapes and colours everything else I say and do. At the top of my list it should say, 'I will live each day in the light of the Christ Child and in the power of God's radical love.' May it be so. Amen.

A Time for Action:

There's a difference between "love" and "God's radical love." Choose a faithful way of living God's radical love this Christmas (volunteering, supporting a neighbour, making peace with an "enemy," righting a wrong, joining a protest, etc. etc.) and take action. Remember, radical love doesn't begin and end with Christmas. It seeks peace, justice, and reconciliation, and the time it takes is the time it takes.

Week 52: Building on Four Strong Pillars

A couple of weeks ago you may have noticed that our devotional did a little "trash talking" about the four great pillars of Christmas: hope, peace, joy, and love. We observed that at Christmas these great icons of the faith are treated as little more than sugary fluff, another decoration to enhance our enjoyment of the season. Banners fly, children's stories abound, and sermons are written about the great pillars. But, is anyone really listening? The dearth of common decency we find in our society day by day suggests a willful deafness to the bedrock messages of hope, peace, joy, and love.

But, is all nobility lost? Must the four pillars be relegated to the scrap heap of fruitless philosophy? Is there a way to transform the pre-Christmas sugar of hope, peace, joy, and love into a heartier post-Christmas meal that feeds a hunger for faithful action in the year to come? Perhaps our banners celebrating hope, peace, joy, and love should be pinned to the walls on January 1st, not December 1st to affirm that they're commitments, not Christmas baubles.

"Everyone then who hears these words of mine and acts on them will be like a wise man who built his house on rock. The rain fell, the floods came, and the winds blew and beat on that house, but it did not fall, because it had been founded on rock. And everyone who hears these words of mine and does not act on them will be like a foolish man who

built his house on sand. The rain fell, and the floods came, and the winds blew and beat against that house, and it fell—and great was its fall!" (Matthew 7: 24-27)

A Personal Journey:

Each Christmas at my local church we spend some time focusing on what I like to call "the four pillars" of the season. On the four Sundays before Christmas Day we focus in turn on Hope, Peace, Joy, and Love because we believe that Jesus Christ embodies each one and offers each one to a hurting world.

Now, just after Christmas, it feels like the world is starting to shift gears already. The great hype and hoopla leading up to Christmas are fading now and soon our thoughts will be turning to the celebration of a new year. You can sense the landscape starting to change as we race away from Christmas. The season of "peace on earth, goodwill towards men and women everywhere" is officially closed. Come back next year!

OK, so the world is moving on. But, I'm not prepared to leave all of Christmas behind in the dust of fond remembrance. I want to bring four presents with me into the new year. As a brand new year dawns this week, I wish myself, and I wish you, the four pillars of the Christmas season. May we all live out this year with an abundance of hope, peace, joy, and love.

I wish us hope. This can be a tough world. Every one of us has our pain and our struggles. Inevitably, even for those of us who are generally happy, there will be hard times. There will be losses. People will be lost to us. Opportunities will pass us by. I wish us hope—not the ability to ignore the tough times—but the ability to work through them and come out healthy on the other side. I wish us the ability to both give and receive hope.

I wish us peace. There is so much violence in the world, from the subtle ways we mistreat those we dislike to the unbridled bloodshed of wars and conflicts worldwide that are so persistent they rarely rate a mention in the news anymore. I wish us acceptance, respect, and tolerance. I wish us justice. May we each have the strength to receive peace in our own lives and to help find peace for others.

I wish us joy. I wish for us the ability to laugh. And, may we always greet life with a sense of awe; with a child's sense of wonder. This is still very much a world filled with good things. People build houses for total strangers, the sick are comforted, the hungry are fed, and justice is done. People make uncommon sacrifices to help one another. The natural world around us is a gift that lifts the soul. I wish us the ability to feel joy and to share it with others.

I wish us love. I wish us the kind of love that's built on a foundation of caring and concern; a love that knows us in the deepest, most muddled and confused places and holds us anyway—especially when we feel unlovable. In this new year, may we experience the gift of being known and accepted. May love make us vital and alive, may it encourage us to celebrate who we are, and may it lead us to be everything we can be. I wish us the ability to both give and receive this love.

It's a short run from Christmas to New Years. We make it every year. Not much choice, really. But, I think it's a shame when Christmas gets taken down, boxed up like an old wreath, and consigned to the basement for another year.

There are Christmas gifts that mean the world to us as we stand on the edge of a brand new year. The greatest of these gifts are hope, peace, joy, and love. May we keep them close to our hearts every minute that God gives us in this amazing world.

A Time for Reflection:

What is "hope" for you as you stand on the edge of a new year? Be specific. What are you hoping for and why?

What is "peace" for you as you stand on the edge of a new year? Describe the "peace" you need. What can you do to achieve it?

What is "joy" for you as you stand on the edge of a new year? Name some of the things that give you joy. Name some of the things that take it away.

What is "love" for you as you stand on the edge of a new year? Be specific. How do you want to love? How do you want to be loved?

When you name your needs for hope, peace, joy, and love where do you see God in this "naming?" What does God's presence mean to you?

A Time for Prayer:

Gracious God, we thank you from the deepest wells of our spirit for the gifts of hope, peace, joy, and love. Guide us to treat them with respect, not as window dressing, and not as the sugar-sweet palaver of a passing season. Hope, peace, joy, and love are your gifts, embodied in your son Jesus, and if we follow their trail we will find your kingdom. These things we know, dear God. Help us to believe them. Amen.

A Time for Action:

Walk with God, and when you know what you're hoping for, listen for the ways you can make it happen. Walk with God, and when you know what peace is for you, listen for the ways through which you can have and bring peace. Walk with God, and when you know what joy is for you, listen for the ways to receive it and pass it on. Walk with God, and when you know what love is for you, listen for the ways you must live from that moment on.

About the Author

Dean Salter is an ordained minister, writer, editor, novelist, and publisher currently living in Okotoks, Alberta. His book of short stories, *Willow People*, was published in 2002. His first novel, *Jason Seeley's War*, was published in 2004, and his most recent novel, *Don't Blame the Bear*, arrived on the scene in 2007.

In 2007, Dean retired as a United Church of Canada minister after 27 years of service divided between pastoral ministry and national and regional staff positions.